CONTENTS

Ships in Focus Publications

Correspondence and editorial:
Roy Fenton
18 Durrington Avenue
London SW20 8NT
0181 879 3527
rfenton@rfenton.demon.co.uk

Orders and photographic:
John & Marion Clarkson
18 Franklands, Longton
Preston PR4 5PD
01772 612855

Printed by Amadeus Press Ltd., Huddersfield.
Designed by Hugh Smallwood, John Clarkson and Roy Fenton.
SHIPS IN FOCUS RECORD
ISBN 1 901 703 02 9

SHIPS IN FOC

With this issue we are pleased contributors. With his knowled south east, Ken Garrett has compi which gives some fascinating i operation of a small fleet. Captain Stephen Carter describes a wreck off the Lizard which, although it caused no immediate casualties, eventually led to a tragedy involving the man who salvaged it. Captain A.W. Kinghorn has contributed an evocative article about the River Tyne in the immediate post-war period, which takes the place of the port history article in this issue.

Record 8 brings us to the end of our notional second volume - notional because, although the words 'Volume 2' appear nowhere, our page numbers run through four issues, and in every fourth issue we include an index. To accommodate the index, we expand this issue by eight pages - a small bonus for loyal followers.

The end of our "second" volume raises the issue of binding *Record.* Once again, Mr. R. Smith, Nullisec, Main Road, Chattenden, Rochester, Kent ME3 8LW offers to bind four issues with gold embossing for £15 including return postage to an address in the UK. Please send your copies direct to him with cheques for £15 made payable to 'The Bindery'. Mr. Smith estimates that orders will take about six weeks. Readers have been very pleased with their bound copies of the first volume. Those who do not have issues 1 to 4 are reminded that we can offer them in bound editions: see our 'house' ad inside the front cover of this issue.

Roy Fenton John Clarkson
February 1999

SUBSCRIPTION RATES FOR THREE ISSUES
Subscribers make a saving on the postage of three issues, and receive each *Record* just as soon as it is published. They are also eligible for concessions on newly-published *Ships in Focus* titles. Readers can start their subscription with *any* issue, and are welcome to backdate it to receive previous issues.

UK	£20	–
Europe (airmail)	£22	–
Rest of world (surface mail)	£22	US$36
Rest of world (airmail)	£30	US$49

Johnston Warren Lines' DROMORE - see letter on page 248.

HOWICK HALL see p198.

TWO-FUNNEL CARGO LINERS
Part Two

DANISH FRUITERS

FRUTERA
Akt. Burmeister & Wain, Copenhagen, Denmark; 1902, 1,536gt, 250 feet
From about 1890, the banana trades from the Caribbean to US Gulf and north eastern ports were served predominantly by small Norwegian steamers, so that in 1893 no fewer than 59 out of 79 ships in the trade flew the Norwegian flag. This led Burmeister & Wain of Copenhagen to build a series of nine reefers for the banana trade, five for Norwegian owners and four for German, and all for charter to United Fruit.

All four German ships and one of the Norwegian vessels, FRUTERA, had two funnels. It is unclear why there was a difference: the two-funnelled FRUTERA had two Scotch boilers, but so did the other Norwegians, and some of the series had three boilers. Built for Conrad Blumer Hofgaard of Christiania, FRUTERA carried three other names and had three other Norwegian owners in her relatively short life. In 1914 she became SJOA, and in 1915 VIKA for just a month before becoming EIDSVOLD. She was torpedoed by U 151 off the coast of Virginia on 4th June 1918 - one of the few successful U-boat operations in US waters during the First World War. *[William Schell]*

BOUND BROOK
Akt. Burmeister & Wain, Copenhagen, Denmark; 1903, 1,515gt, 250 feet
Strictly speaking, the four German fruiters built to the same overall design as FRUTERA should be excluded from this feature, as they were designed to carry 26 passengers. However, BOUND BROOK has been included to complete the story. She was sold in 1911 by original owner H.H. Schmidt of Hamburg to C. Bech & Co., Tvedestrand, Norway. In 1913 she became the BERENICE and survived under this name and several Italian owners until broken up early in 1923.

The German two-funnel fruiters were not long lived. Also built for H.H. Schmidt, BREWSTER (1,517/1903), was wrecked near Cape Hatteras on 28th November 1909 whilst on a voyage from Port Antonio to New York with a cargo of fruit. Of a pair owned by Max Jebsen, BAKER (1,930/1903) was wrecked on Colorados Reef, Cuba on 2nd February 1908 during a voyage from Philadelphia to Puerto Barrios with coal and general cargo. Jebsen's other fruiter, BRADFORD (1,932/1904), had the most adventurous career of the quartet. Renamed HANNA in 1911 she was sold almost immediately to the Turkish Government, who renamed her SIVIN and then DERNA. In a decidedly shady operation, she was landing rifles and ammunition at Tripoli in Libya in October 1911 when scuttled to avoid capture by Italian warships. The Italians themselves raised and took possession of her, and used her under the name BENGASI as a naval transport until she was sold for scrap in 1925. *[William Schell]*

SIKH
Napier and Miller Ltd., Glasgow; 1903, 5,020gt, 401 feet
Gellatley, Hankey and Co. deserve to be better known, if only because of their involvement in the Mogul Line, a competitor to Alfred Holt which mounted a serious legal challenge to the conference system championed by Holts. No published history of the company has been found, yet this photograph of SIKH suggests they had handsome and impressive vessels. She was owned by the Mogul Steamship Co. Ltd. and – unusually – registered at Rochester. Germany seemed to have had an appetite for two-funnel ships, and SIKH was sold to Hamburg Amerika Linie in 1912 and renamed ALMERIA. She was caught in Antwerp in August 1914 and remained there until the end of the First World War. Taken over by the Shipping Controller in 1919, she was initially managed by Turner, Brightman and Co. of London without change of name. In 1921 she was sold to Hajee M.H. Nemazee of Hong Kong and renamed ARMANESTAN in 1923 and, after a change of heart in 1928, became ARABESTAN. She was broken up at Osaka, Japan late in 1931. *[Peter Newall collection]*

TABARISTAN
D. and W. Henderson and Co. Ltd., Glasgow; 1907, 3,883gt, 390 feet
It is not known why Frank Strick built just one two-funneller, although it may be that she was ordered by someone else and Strick - who was always ready to buy and sell contracts - bought her before launching. Certainly she was a solid, if not elegant, vessel. The Admiralty bought TABARISTAN from Strick in 1913 and slowly converted her to a destroyer depot ship: but she was not commissioned as HMS DILIGENCE until 1915. In 1926 she was broken up at Blyth by Hughes Bolckow. *[World Ship Society]*

LATER ZWEISCHORNSTEINERS

GRIEF ex GUBEN (top)
Neptunwerft, Rostock, Germany; 1914, 4,750gt, 420 feet.
Thirteen years after the last *Zweischornsteiner* was launched at Flensburg, another emerged from Rostock, the GUBEN. But her career, both as a merchant ship and in total, was tragically short. The outbreak of war meant her completion proceeded rather slowly, and in 1915 the German Navy took her over as an auxiliary cruiser, naming her SMS GRIEF. She seems a remarkably inept choice for this role, which would require some deception to pass British patrols and to lull victims into a false sense of security, as most ships of her profile were German. As this photograph shows, no effort was made to disguise her second funnel. The Royal Navy's Northern Patrol seems to have had little difficulty in catching her, and in the northern North Sea on 23rd January 1916 she was sunk by a force which included the armed merchant cruisers HMS ANDES and ALCANTARA, the cruiser HMS COMUS and two destroyers. *[Foto Dröppel, courtesy Franz Vonarb]*

LENNEP (second down) and
BRANT COUNTY (third down and bottom)
Neptunwerft, Rostock, Germany; 1915, 4,750gt, 420 feet
The line of *Zweischornsteiners* came to an end with DADG's LENNEP, seen here as she was being completed at Rostock. Laurence Dunn records that her original name was to have been MULHAUSEN, in conformity with DADG's tradition of commemorating German cities. He proposes that the change to LENNEP - the name of a Dutch novelist - indicates a possible sale to Holland early in the First World War.

LENNEP never sailed for the Dutch, but eventually became well known under the Norwegian flag. She was ceded to the UK in 1919 and the Shipping Controller placed her management with F.C. Strick and Co. Ltd. In March 1921, whilst at Swansea, she was bought by J. Coull and Sons, Newcastle-upon-Tyne who renamed her BRANT COUNTY. This name, of a Canadian county, reflected her charter to Intercontinental Transport Services Ltd. – the County Line – which in May 1921 began a service between the St. Lawrence and ports in Continental Europe. BRANT COUNTY's funnel – red base, white band and black top – was that of Canada Steamship Lines Ltd. of Montreal who founded County Line.

In September 1921, BRANT COUNTY was sold by her Newcastle owners to Det Bergenske D/S, suggesting that, in purchasing the ship from the British Government, Coull and Sons were acting on behalf of the Norwegian company. The Bergen company's largest ship, BRANT COUNTY continued running on charter to the Canadian line, making European calls at Hamburg, Rotterdam, Antwerp and Le Havre. A long period of stability was brought to an end by U 757 which torpedoed and sank BRANT COUNTY in the North Atlantic on 11th March 1943. *[Top to bottom: Arnold Kludas collection; World Ship Photo Library collection; Peter Newall collection]*

CHARLES DUNN

HOWICK HALL (page 194)
William Hamilton and Co. Ltd., Port Glasgow; 1910, 4,923gt, 413 feet
Charles G. Dunn and Co. Ltd. are one of the more obscure Liverpool cargo liner companies, probably because their later steamers hardly visited their home port. Captain Charles Dunn became a partner in Herron, Dunn and Co. in 1882, leaving towards the end of the decade to trade alone, initially with some large sailing ships. Steamers were soon added, and at some point Captain Dunn began providing ships for the New York and South America Line.

HOWICK HALL was built for the service between the east coast of the US and the west coast of South America, and her twin funnels may well have been intended to impress the charterers, or shippers, emphasising that they had a powerful modern ship. She was certainly up-to-date in design, and Laurence Dunn records that she was one of the first cargo liners with longitudinal framing. Her deck outfit included a derrick capable of 35-ton lifts. The grey hull was still an unusual feature in 1910 and, with funnels whose yellow bases were separated from black tops by red and blue bands carrying white diamonds, she certainly looked impressive.

Not long after the outbreak of the First World War, HOWICK HALL and three other Dunn ships were sold to the United States Steel Products Co. Inc., a subsidiary of the United States Steel Corporation. It is quite possible that US Steel money was behind the South American service all along, and that the purchase of the four British ships in the Autumn of 1914 was to help safeguard them both from attack by German warships and from requisition by the British Government. At the same time US Steel also bought another British company, Isthmian Steamship Co. Ltd., and were to retain the word 'Isthmian' in company names for many years.

HOWICK HALL continued in US service without change of her rather British-sounding name until October 1929, when she returned to the Red Ensign as DOVENDEN, owned by the Exeter Shipping Co. Ltd. Laurence Dunn records that DOVENDEN was idle almost continuously, first at New York and later in Rotterdam until January 1935, when sold to Ditta Luigi Pittaluga Vapori of Genoa. Pittaluga's fleet is worthy of further study, as over the years it comprised a remarkable number of former British cargo liners. Pittaluga bought DOVENDEN ostensibly for scrap, but then returned her to service as IRCANIA, before selling her to further Italian owners in 1937. These owners seemed a little careless of their old ship, and in June 1940 she was in Jacksonville, Florida when Italy finally joined what Mussolini thought was to be the winning side in the Second World War. The IRCANIA remained laid up and was taken over by the US Maritime Commission in June 1941. Renamed RACELAND, despite her age, she was selected for arduous service. On a voyage that should have taken her from Boston via Reykjavik to Murmansk, she was sunk by German aircraft north of Bear Island on 28th March 1942. She was a straggler from convoy PQ13 which had been scattered by bad weather.

In the photograph on page 194, HOWICK HALL flies a US courtesy flag from her foremast, although the background and the ship's pristine condition suggests it was taken during trials on the Clyde. It was the discovery of this photo that inspired the editors to research this article. The photograph reminded us of Laurence Dunn's fine painting and description of HOWICK HALL in his *Merchant Ships of the World in Colour 1910-1929*, a book which anybody who has photographic captions to write should study closely. We would be delighted to hear from anyone who has photographs of HOWICK HALL under later colours or as DOVENDEN, IRPINIA or RACELAND.

CROFTON HALL (below, opposite top) and **COMMERCIAL TRAVELLER** (opposite bottom)
William Hamilton and Co. Ltd., Port Glasgow; 1913, 5,774gt, 405 feet
In the photograph below, CROFTON HALL looks just a little too good to be true, and the original negative (this is from a copy) may have seen some retouching. Nevertheless, it is an important view of Dunns' last ship built for the New York and South America Line. She is a development of HOWICK HALL, although the earlier ship's combined bridge deck and forecastle has given way to a long bridge deck. The accommodation has been increased, giving rise to suspicions that she may have carried a complement of passengers which, technically, puts her beyond our definition of a cargo liner.

As with HOWICK HALL, she was bought by United States Steel Products Co. Inc. in 1914 and, after lengthy service, was transferred to their Isthmian Steamship Co. Ltd. in 1931 (opposite top). Two years later she was sold to Moore & McCormack Co. Inc. and became COMMERCIAL TRAVELLER. The photograph of her under this name, kindly supplied by William Schell, is of considerable historic interest, as the name was kept for barely a year. Apparent changes, which have occurred since she was built 20 years earlier, include the loss of ventilators on the forecastle and addition of a crow's-nest, to which a seamen is ascending.

In 1934 COMMERCIAL TRAVELLER was sold to the Colombian Navy for use as a naval training ship. As CUCUTA she survived in this, presumably sedentary, role until 1957 when she was towed from Central America to Hamburg for scrap, arriving on 4th March 1957 to be cut up by Eckhardt & Co. Quite possibly, this was the only occasion since new that she had been in European waters. *[Opposite top: Peter Newall collection; bottom: William Schell]*

CROFTON HALL

COMMERCIAL TRAVELER
MOORE & Mc CORMACK

NORWEGIAN MOTORSHIPS

SUD-AMERICANO (top) and **WESER** (bottom)
Deutsche Werke Kiel A.G., Kiel, Germany; 1929, 6,660gt, 461 feet
The Norwegian motorships SUD-AMERICANO and SUD-EXPRESO emerged with an enormous flourish, yet few ships could have been such a disappointment to their owners, builders and charterers. They were planned to be the fastest motor cargo liners yet built, and on trials achieved very creditable speeds of around 18 knots. Their intended use was the New York to River Plate service of Linea Sud Americana S.A., a service jointly operated by Moore-McCormack Lines and Ivar An. Christensen of Oslo. The latter still operates services between North and South America as Ivarans Rederi.

The novel feature of these ships, and what turned out to be their Achilles' heel, was machinery by their German builder: double-acting, two-stroke diesels. These engines did not meet expectations, and the owners refused to take delivery of the ships. SUD-AMERICANO remained at Kiel as SCHLESWIG, and in June 1931 – two years after she had undergone trials – she was taken over by a trust, Deutsche Revisions und Treuhandbank A.G. She made at least one voyage with her original engines, on charter to Blue Star as YAKIMA STAR in September 1931, afterwards returning to lay-up in Kiel. In 1934 she was sold to Norddeutscher Lloyd and re-engined with two seven-cylinder MAN diesels, and emerged with only one funnel as WESER.

WESER was in Central America at the outbreak of war in 1939 and was taken over by the Kriegsmarine as a supply ship for the auxiliary cruiser ORION. But after a year in this role WESER was captured by the Canadian armed merchant cruiser PRINCE RUPERT on 29th September 1940 and put into Canadian service as VANCOUVER ISLAND. However, on 15th October 1941 U 558 put an end to her varied career when she torpedoed VANCOUVER ISLAND about 750 miles west of Fastnet.
[Bottom: Peter Newall collection]

SUD-EXPRESO (top), **WENATCHEE STAR** (middle) and **ELBE** (bottom)
Deutsche Werke Kiel A.G., Kiel, Germany; 1929, 6,660gt, 461 feet
SUD-EXPRESO was completed in July 1929 but, like her sister, she was returned to her builders as being too slow. After lay-up in Kiel as HOLSTEIN, she too was sold to a trust who chartered her to Blue Star for at least one voyage, for which she was renamed WENATCHEE STAR, before returning to lay up in Kiel. In 1934 Norddeutscher Lloyd bought her, gave her diesels similar to those of her sister and, as ELBE, she began a short but useful life.

In September 1939 ELBE took refuge in the then neutral port of Yokohama, Japan. After over 18 months of idleness, she sailed from Dairen on 4th April 1941 with a cargo of rubber hoping to break the Allied blockade of German ports. However, off the Cape Verde Islands on 6th June she was found by Swordfish from HMS EAGLE and sunk. *[Middle: Laurence Dunn; bottom: Peter Newall collection]*

CUNARDERS

SILVERPLANE (top), **ALSATIA** (middle) and **UNION FREEDOM** (bottom)

J.L. Thompson & Sons Ltd., Sunderland; 1948, 7,226gt, 483 feet

The last examples of cargo liners with two funnels made little pretence that one stack was a dummy. Placed right forward on the bridge, the fore funnel could not have served the boilers of these turbine-driven ships, and instead accommodated the radar equipment, the monkey island, chart room, radio room, wheel house and quarters for both the master and a pilot.

The ships were ordered by S.J. Thompson & Co., whose family also owned the Sunderland yard in which they were built, as part of ambitious plans to expand their Silver Line fleet. These plans included three other turbine-driven cargo vessels which were sold before completion to Alfred Holt. SILVERPLANE and SILVERBRIAR were intended for a round-the-world service, for which their three turbines drove them at a creditable 16 knots. But the service did not prosper and the pair was sold in 1951 to Cunard for their North Atlantic services. SILVERPLANE became ALSATIA and operated largely on the London, Le Havre and New York service. Their two-funnel profile was unique for pure cargo ships in post-war years, and gave them a distinction amongst the shipping fraternity. Surprisingly, their traditional-sounding names had not been used previously by Cunard.

In 1963 Cunard sold the pair to C.Y. Tung who registered them in Taiwan under the ownership of China Union Lines. ALSATIA became UNION FREEDOM and gave long and useful service in the Far East. She was not broken up until 1977, when she arrived at Taiwan on 11th March for demolition by the Nan Fu Steel Corporation Ltd. *[Top: Alex Duncan, George Scott collection]*

SILVERBRIAR (top) and **ANDRIA** (bottom)
J.L. Thompson & Sons Ltd., Sunderland; 1948, 7,226gt, 483 feet
It is notable how many sister ships had careers which, although comprising several phases, ran in parallel. SILVERBRIAR (seen at Vancouver) marched in step with her sister SILVERPLANE, becoming Cunard's ANDRIA in 1951, and China Union Lines' UNION FAITH in 1963. However, tragedy struck on 6th April 1969. UNION FAITH was inward bound for New Orleans in the Mississippi with general cargo from Hong Kong when she collided with a string of oil barges. She caught fire and sank the next day, and 25 of her crew lost their lives. *[Top: Ivor Rooke collection]*

Note. As we stated in the introduction to the first part of this article, it is usually only possible to identify two-funnel cargo liners from photographs or descriptions, and it is possible that some have been missed in preparing this feature. We would be pleased to hear about others – especially if photographs can be supplied. However, we would remind readers that we are only considering cargo liners with limited accommodation for passengers – the British definition was just twelve – and with funnels in line amidships.

THE LOSS OF THE CAPITAINE REMY

Captain Stephen Carter and Paul Richards

On 28th November 1920 a five-masted wooden auxiliary schooner had rounded the Longships and was proceeding up the Channel bound for Nantes. The weather was steadily worsening into a severe south easterly gale. The CAPITAINE REMY, barely two years old, had been built by the Foundation Shipbuilding Company of Portland, Oregon in 1918. The vessel grossed 1,853 tons and had loaded a cargo of 2,500 tons of coal at Barry Docks. Equipped with a pair of triple-expansion steam engines which produced 68 NHP, she was a large schooner (259 x 45 x 22 feet) owned by the French Government and registered in Bordeaux. She was one of a number of vessels purchased to import coal into the war-ravaged country.

By the early hours of the following day CAPITAINE REMY was fighting for survival 14 miles south of the Longships. Her masts had been broken or carried away by the stress of weather, and her engines could not hold her from being blown towards the shore. Fearing the ship might founder, her crew of 38 officers and men took to the boats, securing the painters to the taffrail of the stricken vessel so that they could be slipped quickly in the event of the ship sinking suddenly. The crew were in a terrifying predicament: it appeared that the ship could not remain afloat much longer and they would be adrift in raging seas and driven towards the rocky shore. But fate was with them that night: out of the darkness came a Brixham sailing trawler, one of a type of vessels renowned for their sea-keeping capabilities. With skilful seamanship of the highest calibre, the skipper and crew of the trawler rescued the entire complement of the stricken schooner from their boats and bore away up channel to land the exhausted French crew at Brixham. At the time the trawler left, the schooner had been driven to within four miles of the Lizard and both the rescuers and rescued expected her to be driven onto the rocks or to founder before the gale abated. But, contrary to their expectations, neither happened and the dramatic events of being dismasted and abandoned and the rescue of the crew were only a foretaste of a continuing drama that was to last for nearly four years.

One of the mysteries surrounding this rescue was the identity of the gallant Brixham trawler. In an age when press reporting was usually very accurate one report named her as the ketch VIGILANT (38/1907), but another stated that it was GRATITUDE (59/1903). Perhaps both vessels were involved.

Derelict

A few hours after the crew that been rescued, the little coaster MARENA (303/1908) encountered the derelict CAPITAINE REMY. MARENA had been built for Joseph Monks of Warrington and employed in the Mersey and Irish Sea trades until her sale to a Cardiff shipowner early in 1920, hence her presence in the English Channel. Powered by a 'sewing machine' of a compound engine, coasters like MARENA had barely enough power to move themselves through the water, so towing a large derelict with masts and rigging dragging in the water in atrocious weather was out of the question. But the

CAPITAINE REMY dressed overall, probably just after launching. *[World Ship Photo Library].*

Two of the Fowey Steam Tug Company's vessels: the COUNTESS OF JERSEY, built at Swansea in 1881 and broken up at Penzance in 1934 (right); and the GALLANT (below), built by the Rother Iron Works, Rye in 1884 and surviving in West Country ownership until 1963 when W.J. Reynolds Ltd. broke her up at Laira Bridge. *[Right: Stephen Carter collection].*

crew of the MARENA did recover the ship's papers which had been forgotten by the French crew in their haste to escape.

On 2nd December a steamer reported nearly colliding with a derelict vessel eight miles south-east of the Lizard, and the following morning the collier OAKTOWN (436/1902), running from Swansea for Rouen with coal, limped into Plymouth Sound down by the head and with decks awash having collided with an upturned hulk five miles south-east of the Lizard during the night. For nearly a week the capsized ship drifted in the busy shipping lanes and presented a great danger as it was virtually impossible to detect in the dark. Eventually she was spotted by the coastguards from Polruan who reported her position as ten miles off the Dodman.

Henry Paull

This news quickly reached Henry Arthur Paull, manager of the Fowey Steam Tug Company. In 1920 Alderman Henry Paull was at the height of his business and civic careers, and hoping to become mayor in 1921. He captained the Fowey Fire Brigade, was Vice Consul for Sweden, was a member of the Fowey Harbour Commissioners, and owned two West Country trading smacks, the motorised ketch RIVAL (18/1889) and the sloop RICHARD AND JANE (40/1829). He also had interests in the town's first garage together with his motor engineer son, Arthur Henry Paull, and others.

At this time the Fowey Steam Tug Company operated three tugs: COUNTESS OF JERSEY (40/1881); GALLANT (76/1884, lengthened in 1903); and the wooden-hulled ex-trawler CRUDEN BAY (124/1898). The tugs were owned by various individual shareholders, as was the practice at the time, and the share transactions contained in the registration documents for the first two alone contain

The Fowey Steam Tug Company's largest vessel, the CRUDEN BAY, on a pleasure trip. Built as a trawler at Anstruther in 1889, her wooden hull lasted until 1929 when broken up by W.J. Reynolds at Torpoint. *[Stephen Carter collection].*

enough material for a small volume. Since the turn of the century Henry Paull, together with his wife Maria Florence, his son Arthur, and his brother Albert, a retired farmer, had built up large share holdings in all three tugs and in each case Henry Paull was the managing owner. In 1920, together with Truro solicitor John Messer Bennetts, Henry Paull set up the Fowey Tug and Salvage Company Ltd. although the tugs were to remain in private individual ownership until 1924.

Entry refused

Returning to the derelict, the Fowey Steam Tug Company's largest tug CRUDEN BAY under the command of Captain H. Wyatt set sail immediately, quickly followed by the GALLANT with Captain J. Toms in command and Henry Paull on board. By late morning they had located CAPITAINE REMY, floating upside-down and down by the head. Parts of broken masts and rigging were floating up alongside the hull which made any approach by the tugs potentially hazardous. However, by 1.15 pm the tugs had managed to secure tow ropes to the only accessible place, the A-brackets on the propeller shafts. Towing started towards Fowey but a morse signal was observed from Polruan coastguards forbidding the tow to be brought to Fowey if the draught of the derelict vessel was more than 25 feet. The recently-appointed Harbourmaster, Captain Fred Collins, quickly realised that if the derelict sank or grounded in the main channel of the harbour then the economy of the town and the surrounding district could be very seriously affected. This decision by Captain Collins, described as the presiding genius of modern Fowey by Roland Roddis in his book *Cornish Harbours* (1951), was later to become the centre of some controversy. However, the Harbour Commissioners backed their man.

Henry Paull decided to tow the derelict to Par Bay instead, but progress was very slow. The ship's

The upturned hull of the CAPITAINE REMY being towed by the CRUDEN BAY and GALLANT. *[Paul Richards collection]*

Another view of the towage of the hulk. The propellor of the CAPITAINE REMY and several spars can be seen. *[Paul Richards collection]*

draught was estimated at 32 feet and it was discovered later that one anchor was dragging along the bottom. As the water shallowed the anchor got a better hold and the ship became held fast about one mile from Polkerris beach. As it was then after 8.00 pm towing was abandoned for the day. Both tugs went back to Fowey and returned to Polkerris next morning. Henry Paull had arranged for a diving team to come from Plymouth to assess the problems underwater. Working from small boats the tug crews and some of Paull's men succeeded in cutting free the masts and debris which was floating by the hull. The diving team reported that the ship was being held by her anchor which had dropped out when the ship turned over, and they were instructed by Paull to saw through the links by hand in order to release the anchor and cable from the ship. Once this was accomplished the two tugs tried to tow the wreck further inshore, but they had hardly started when the other anchor slipped out and again the vessel was held fast. Once again the divers had to laboriously cut the links.

Frustration

After much frustration the ship was eventually towed at high water into a position about 300 yards from Polkerris, and at low water much of the upturned hull was exposed. So far the salvage had been reasonably successful if somewhat slow. The tug company appeared to be in possession of a sound ship with modern engines and boilers. All the stern gear and rudder fittings were brass, and there was still the best part of 2,500 tons of coal on board. She represented a valuable asset but she was still upside-down. Over the coming months the salvors were unable to right

The hulk of the CAPITAINE REMY at Polkerris with parbuckling gear rigged. The CRUDEN BAY blows off steam. *[Paul Richards collection]*

Tugs get into position for a righting attempt, from left to right GALLANT, CRUDEN BAY, COUNTESS OF JERSEY and the Admiralty tug ROVER. *[Paul Richards collection]*

the vessel or to lighten her sufficiently to allow her to be moved at a sheltered location at Pont Pill Fowey, where dismantling could take place in an orderly fashion.

Parbuckling failed to right her. This accepted salvage technique uses the reverse principle to that used by a dray man rolling a beer barrel down into a cellar. Photographic evidence suggests that Paull chartered a large Admiralty salvage tug, the ROVER (615dwt/1908). This Plymouth-based tug developed 1,400 horsepower, compared with 210HP and 300HP for CRUDEN BAY and GALLANT respectively, but was not successful. The salvors then tried filling the machinery spaces and forecastle with empty barrels and pumping compressed air into the hull to reduce the draught but this also failed. It was rumoured locally that several major salvage firms had looked at the job and would have nothing to do with it. Costs were mounting rapidly, and to date the only return had been to strip the accessible brasswork from the rudder and propeller shafts.

By September 1921 little had changed and Paull applied officially to his fellow Harbour Commissioners for permission to bring the vessel into Fowey for removal of the engines and boilers before righting her. The Harbourmaster, Captain Collins, had been making his own observations of the wreck and reported to his Commissioners that the ship measured 36 feet from the taffrail to the bottom (or top) of the keel. On the previous set of spring tides the vessel had floated on a draught of 30 feet 6 inches and he was adamant that in his professional opinion the draught must be no more than 25 feet to give sufficient clearance of at least 5 feet over the banks at the entrance to Pont Pill. His fellow Commissioners, led by Sir Arthur Quiller Couch, agreed, and to make matters worse for Paull they asked the tug company to put up a bond of £8,000 in case the vessel sank and blocked the port or was abandoned by them within the port. Raising such a bond was impossible, and Paull accused the Commissioners of putting obstacles in his way. He argued that, if the CAPITAINE REMY was brought into Fowey, it would create considerable employment during a period of depression, but the Commissioners would not be swayed.

Desperate measures

There seemed to be only one option: the use of explosives to blow apart the wreck and gain access to the cargo and machinery. This was fraught with difficulties because explosives were not predictable, and then there was the problem of bringing ashore the engines, boilers and cargo that could be recovered. Originally the engines had been a very saleable commodity, but after 12 months in salt water they were probably worth little more than scrap.

Prior to Captain Collins' appointment as Harbourmaster in April 1919, Henry Paull held the position of Collector of Dues to Fowey Harbour Commissioners and with his other interests he would undoubtedly have had considerable influence on decisions on maritime matters. Without the presence of someone with the strength of character of Captain Collins the final outcome might have been very different. At this stage the story disappears both from the local press and from the minutes of the Harbour Commissioners, but in February 1922 the Registrar of Companies in London was writing to remind the Fowey Tug and Salvage Company Ltd. that they had not submitted their annual returns as required by law for limited companies. Reminders seemed to go unheeded as on 17th August 1923 the Registrar dissolved the company.

At this time the tugs were managed from 6 Fore Street, Fowey, from an office which was within the garage premises owned by the Paulls. However, on the date of dissolution of the limited company these tugs were still owned by individual shareholders and were still operated by the Fowey Steam Tug Company, which was not a limited company. Henry

The upturned hulk moored to large buoys at Polkerris during attempts to lighten its draught. The air lines can be clearly seen. *[Paul Richards collection]*

Paull was the manager. Not until 24th March 1924 were the three tugs transferred into the ownership of the Fowey Tug and Salvage Company Ltd. so presumably the directors and probably the solicitor, John Messer Bennetts, had managed to have the company reinstated.

Prior to the transactions of March 1924 Henry Paull made some surprising moves. In February he transferred his shareholdings in the COUNTESS OF JERSEY and the GALLANT to his brother Albert Paull and his solicitor John Messer Bennetts. Two months later his shareholding in the CRUDEN BAY was also transferred. The transfer of the three tugs to the limited company meant that Henry Paull no longer had any personal ownership interest in the vessels. At about the same time his son Arthur Henry mortgaged his shareholdings in the GALLANT and the COUNTESS OF JERSEY for £300 and £150 respectively, the mortgagee being none other than the renowned Plymouth shipowner, Albert Westacott, who set a staggering interest rate of 20% at a time when banks were lending at between 3% and 5%.

As soon as the three tugs were registered with the Fowey Tug and Salvage Company Ltd. they were all immediately mortgaged for £4,750 at an interest rate of 10%. This time the mortgagee was John Wheeler Higman, a local china clay merchant from Polgray, St. Austell.

Tragedy

The last chapter in this sad saga opened on Monday, 10th November 1924 when news of Henry Paull's tragic death reached the burgers of Fowey as they assembled at the Town Hall to install the new mayor, Mr G. Varco. On that morning as father and son went to the Fore Street garage Henry Paull told his son that he was feeling seedy; and at the subsequent inquest Arthur Paull stated that his father had been unwell for two years and had had 'plenty of worries' during that time. Was this a reference to the CAPITAINE REMY affair? At the inquest Cyril Rickard, whose premises adjoined the tug company office in Fore Street, said that just before 11.00 am on 10th November he heard an explosion but took no immediate action as he thought it might be a car backfiring in the garage. However, a few minutes later he smelt gunpowder and went to investigate and found Charles Hunkin in a passageway. Hunkin, a rigger from Boddinick employed by the tug company reported that he and Arthur Paull went into the office and found Henry Paull sitting in a chair with his head leaning on the window sill. His hand was resting on an electric exploder, an instrument used to set off explosives underwater. The exploder was attached by wires to a detonator in his employer's mouth and the explosion had blown away his face. Arthur ran for a doctor, but his father was already dead. Dr Drew Drury, who had attended the deceased for several years, stated that Henry Paull had been very depressed and worried for some time.

Henry Paull left letters to several family members, but their full content was not revealed at the inquest. Now, after the passage of so much time, the precise nature of the problems which beset Henry Paull and his associates will never be known. What can be deduced, however, is that at first the CAPITAINE REMY may have seemed like a gift from the Gods for the shareholders of the Fowey Tug Company. But the slump in shipping prices, coupled with the subsequent failure of the company to salvage the ship successfully, dramatically changed its fortunes. It is known that Paull had been negotiating with the French Government, presumably to gain some compensation for removing a dangerous obstacle from the busy shipping lane, but we do not know what success he had.

The wreck of CAPITAINE REMY was eventually blown apart and the engines and boilers were salvaged. Part of the deck was towed into Fowey to lie on the beach opposite the china clay jetties, but is is extremely unlikely that the monies realised for what had become mere scrap came anywhere near to the costs of mounting the salvage operations.

The problems which beset Henry Paull and his tug company did not prevent the town turning out for his funeral. On the following Thursday Fowey Congregational Church, where Paull had worshipped for over 40 years, was full: the mayor and corporation turned out in full regalia and most of the town's prominent citizens appear in the list of the mourners together with family, friends and employees. His death, at the age of 63, ended a long and active career. As well as his 30-year connection with the tug company, Henry Paull is remembered as a leading instigator of the campaign to regain Fowey's borough charter in 1913, and as man with many and varied interests.

Survival

And what became of CAPITAINE REMY? After the removal of her engines and boilers she seemed almost indestructible. The machinery was dropped to the bottom, towed into Fowey by CRUDEN BAY and scrapped. But the hull seemed rooted to the sea bed. After every gale local inhabitants expected the vessel to be smashed up and her timbers washed ashore, but no. CAPITAINE REMY remained on Polkerris beach like a half-tide rock. Some of her originally salvaged spars were used as shore derricks at Brazen Island Shipyard, and for years there was talk of using the Fowey grab dredger to recover some of her cargo of coal which had spilled onto the seabed. But nothing happened until the beginning of the Second World War when the wreck was finally demolished by explosives and the remaining timbers were towed ashore between Par and Polkerris and cut up for firewood. Many of the iron fittings were taken into Fowey and dumped near Brazen Island in Pont Pill with the Harbour Commissioners' old mooring buoys and chains. These remnants finally went for scrap in the early 1960s when the Commissioners had a tidy up, but it is said that on a good day the outline of the ship can still be seen in the sand from the top of the cliffs at Polkerris.

Did Henry Paull himself become a casualty of the CAPITAINE REMY nearly four years after she was abandoned? Those reading this account must draw their own conclusions.

BRITISH YARD, GREEK TRAMP

Roy Fenton

There is a popular perception of the Greek tramp as being a down-at-heel second-hand purchase, passed on by British or other owners as being super-annuated and uneconomic. The photographs here are chosen to counter that image, all showing tramps built in the 1950s by British yards for Greek owners. These were by no means untypical: a quick survey of building output in that decade reveals at least sixty such hulls built in the UK whilst, as the fifties wore on, Dutch, French, German, Japanese and Yugoslav yards contributed similar tramps to the Greek-controlled fleet.

A secondary purpose of this feature is to emphasise that Greeks have often had long and interesting careers as shipowners. Many of the older-established companies had or still have offices in the UK, and are part of this country's shipping history. They are well worth studying, and the secrecy which surrounds some Greek shipowning families adds to the interest of the chase. Greeks are now the world's biggest shipowners. They did not get there by accident, and their traditions and methods are worthy subjects for the maritime historian.

EMBIRICOS OWNED AND MANAGED

The shipowning interests of the Embiricos clan of Andros have been extensive and very complex. By 1910, Embiricos Brothers controlled a fleet of 22 ships, including the first of three transAtlantic liners, PATRIS (2,558/1909). Stamatios G. Embiricos was one of the first Greek owners to set up a limited company to finance his ships in order to encourage small investors to put money into his venture. S.G. Embiricos Ltd. dates from about 1897 and built several tramps in the UK, including the GEORGE M. EMBIRICOS (5,728/1921), and an earlier STAMATIOS G. EMBIRICOS (3,941/1936), both by Short Brothers at Sunderland. Since 1991 the Embiricos shipping interests have been consolidated under Andros Maritime Agencies Ltd., with offices in London and Athens.

STAMATIOS G. EMBIRICOS (top)
Wm. Doxford and Sons (Shipbuilders) Ltd., Sunderland; 1956, 8,878gt, 486 feet
With strong maritime traditions, Greek owners maintained some customs that had fallen into neglect elsewhere. Both funnel and hull of the STAMATIOS G. EMBIRICOS bear what are undoubtedly mourning bands, probably in blue. It is likely that this is in honour of George S. Embiricos – the founder's son – who is listed as being responsible for the ship in contemporary editions of *Lloyds Confidential Index.*

This Doxford motorship had a remarkably simple career. She was formally owned by the Edina Compania Naviera S.A. whose brass plate was in Panama, although the ship resolutely flew the Greek flag, as in this photograph. She was laid up at Eleusis on 5th October 1981, and seemingly did not sail again until a Piraeus company bought her in 1985, renamed her SWORD, and almost immediately resold her to breakers in Bangladesh. She arrived at Chittagong on 27th November 1985.

DORIS (bottom)
Cammell Laird & Co. (Shipbuilders & Engineers) Ltd., Birkenhead; 1954, 6,042gt, 470 feet
Cammell Laird built a remarkable variety of ships – from tugs to submarines, and from paddle steamers to aircraft carriers – but completed very few tramps. In 1954, however, they turned out the motor vessel DORIS which was registered in Liberia by the eponymous Doris Compania Naviera S.A., Panama. Ultimate owners were Z.L. and G.L. Cambanis, who entrusted management to S.G. Embiricos Ltd., which explains the white ribbon on the grey hull. The Cambanis brothers were never large owners, and their black funnel with white band and blue ball has graced only a handful of ships. DORIS made occasional visits to the river on which she was built, and these continued after she had been sold to L.M. Valmas & Son in 1973 and renamed IRIS. IRIS was sold again in 1981, to become KASTRO K, and after a brief spell as STEPON in 1984 arrived at Gadani Beach to be demolished on 25th May 1984.

LYKIARDOPULO

The Lykiardopulo family of Cephalonia are regarded as being 'traditional' shipowners, probably because they continue to finance their relatively modest fleet in time-honoured ways, without recourse to such measures as bank loans taken out on the strength of time-charters for ships not yet built. Founder of the company was Nikolaos D. Lykiardopulo (1866-1963), his longevity no doubt influencing his successor's policies. However, Lykiardopulo did innovate, the family being amongst those who bought the seven T2-type tankers offered to Greece by the US Government in 1948. Not quite the first Greek tankers, these purchases nevertheless led the way to the phenomenal growth of the Greek-controlled tanker fleet. As Lykiardopulo & Co. Ltd., the family now control four large tankers and two bulkers, one of which carries the traditional name DAPHNE (35,476/1984).

DAPHNE
William Gray & Co. Ltd., West Hartlepool; 1954, 5,779gt, 458 feet
With her split superstructure and tall funnel, DAPHNE looks like a ship built for a traditional owner, and it is no surprise that she has a triple-expansion steam engine. Her design is a development of that of MERCHANT DUKE (5,891/1951), built by Gray for the Drake Shipping Co. Ltd. – Lykiardopulo's British-flag company.

DAPHNE was built for the Daphne Steamship Co. S.A. of Liberia, but moved to the Greek flag in 1960. In 1969 Lykiardopulo sold her to Italian owners as MONTONE, and only three years later she went to breakers at La Spezia. However, she was reprieved, put under the Panama flag and survived until 1977. On 9th April she grounded south of Carrara whilst leaving that port from Augusta and was abandoned by her crew. The wreck was sold to Italian breakers, who commenced demolishing it in September. There are good photographs of MONTONE on pages 282 and 327 of *Marine News* for 1977.

Note that in this photograph DAPHNE is unusual for a Greek-owned ship in flying a houseflag, Lykiardopulo's white with a red star, which also appears on her black-topped yellow funnel. DAPHNE and NYMPHE were frequent visitors to British ports in the late 1960s.

NYMPHE
Furness Shipbuilding Co. Ltd., Haverton Hill-on-Tees; 1954, 5,653gt, 467 feet
It seems odd that Lykiardopulo should have taken delivery of two such different ships in the same year, the Tees-built NYMPHE being a motor vessel with a profile quite distinct from that of DAPHNE. Perhaps the association with Furness Shipbuilding Co. Ltd. dated from their building the motor tanker MERCHANT BARON (12,102/1953) for Lykiardopulo's Drake Shipping. NYMPHE was by no means the family's first motor ship, as just before the war they had taken delivery of one of the first Greek-owned diesel tramps, Doxford's MERCHANT PRINCE (5,229/1939). The design of NYMPHE was developed further, and MERCHANT ROYAL (9,772/1957) was completed by Blythswood with a similar profile apart from a much shorter forecastle. In 1959 and 1960 Livanos' Trent Maritime took delivery of three ships from Furness which, at 517 feet, were developments of the NYMPHE design.

Not surprisingly, NYMPHE had a longer career with Lykiardopulo than her steam fleet mate, although her end came almost contemporaneously. In 1970 she was sold to become VIRGINIA METHENITIS under other Greek owners, who in 1977 renamed her DRYADES. On 4th December of that year she was bound in ballast from Basrah to Volos when she was stranded in heavy weather on the Greek island of Euboea. Declared a constructive total loss, she was sold to be broken up.

CHANDRIS

Chandris is one of the best-known Greek shipowning families largely because of their extensive passenger fleet. But since 1911, when John D. Chandris first became a shipowner, the family have also operated dry cargo and tanker tonnage. These have been distinguished from the cruise ships by a different funnel design, a yellow base separated from a black top by a broad blue band bordered by white and carrying a white X. On passenger ships, the funnel is simply blue with black top and white X. Chandris also had their own British subsidiary, Charlton Shipping Co. Ltd., which wore their colours.

The Greeks proclivity for using their own funnel colours is another example of their pride in their ships, although this can sometimes have amusing consequences. In the 1970s a Chandris tanker went aground near Milford Haven, amid the usual concerns about pollution. Oh no, said a company spokesman, that is not one of our ships, it belongs to a company in Panama. Television views of the tanker, clearly showing her Chandris funnel, told another story.

DONA MARGARITA (top)
Wm. Doxford and Sons (Shipbuilders) Ltd., Sunderland; 1956, 8,716gt, 483 feet
This was one of four motorships built in 1956 and 1957 similar to STAMATIOS G. EMBIRICOS and a series for Bank Line. The first Chandris pair had virtually no forecastle.

DONA MARGARITA had an impressively long career with the Chandris group. Between 1963 and 1966 she ran as MARIRITA, adopting the MARI- name style which Chandris used for ships trading under the Greek flag. Reversion to DONA MARGARITA in 1966 saw her stay with Greek registration until 1972. She was then resolutely Liberian until arrival at Bombay for breaking on 26th June 1981.

DONA EDIE (upper middle)
Wm. Doxford and Sons (Shipbuilders) Ltd., Sunderland; 1957, 9,746gt, 509 feet
The pair of Doxford motorships completed for Chandris in 1957 were larger, this time with a full height forecastle and some other subtle changes, for instance to the kingposts. The effect of the forecastle and the deepening of the white strake gave them an elegance which belied the name tramp.

DONA EDIE was renamed ISOBEL in 1961 and then remained with Chandris until 1981. For a few months she ran as INTRA TRADITION before Bombay breakers claimed her, and she arrived at the Indian port on 21st February 1982.

DONA KATERINA (lower middle)
Wm. Doxford and Sons (Shipbuilders) Ltd., Sunderland; 1957, 9,746gt, 509 feet
The surroundings of Port Chalmers, New Zealand set off the elegant lines of DONA KATERINA very well. Her career was to be spent entirely with Chandris under her original name, although the title of her owning company and her flag changed several times. She too was broken up at Bombay, arriving on 12th October 1981.

MISS CHANDRIS (bottom)
Wm. Doxford and Sons (Shipbuilders) Ltd., Sunderland; 1959, 9,855gt, 509 feet
MISS CHANDRIS represents a further development of the Doxford motorship, with an extra hatch, bipod masts and a slightly more 'streamlined' superstructure. There was a change of naming style too, but clearly within Chandris' predilection for female names.

In this case, handsome was as handsome did, and she gave Chandris excellent service. Renamed GENIE in 1969, she traded until November 1981 when she went into lay up in the Seychelles, an unusual location, where she suffered an explosion and fire in her machinery in December 1982. It was not until January 1985 that she made her way to Karachi and the breakers.

LIVANOS

The Livanos family of Chios is an excellent example of how often only knowledge of funnel colours allows the ownership of a Greek vessel to be assigned. The family's traditional funnel colour is black with a broad white band on which are two Greek key bands or 'meanders', and between them a letter L. The L is red in the case of ships owned by descendants of Stavros G. Livanos (1887-1956) and blue for those who can trace their ancestry back to N.G. Livanos. For Greek flag ships, the L is sometimes replaced with the Greek letter lambda, Λ.

Although a powerful shipowner in his own right, Stavros Livanos is probably best known for having two daughters, Tina and Eugenie, who married shipowning rivals Aristotle Onassis and Stavros Niarchos. Not from traditional shipping familes, these two were seen as impudent young upstarts. But it was such newcomers who gave impetus to the growth of Greek-owned shipping after the war.

ATLANTIC EMPRESS
William Gray & Co. Ltd., West Hartlepool; 1949, 7,310gt, 471 feet
Like many Greeks, Stavros G. Livanos both operated from the UK and had ships built here in post-war years. His London company was Trent Maritime Co. Ltd., whose ships were given names beginning DUKE OF. Freighters and tankers put under the Liberian or Panama flag were usually given names beginning ATLANTIC, reflecting ownership by Atlantic Freighters Ltd. One ship was built in the UK for Atlantic Freighters Ltd., the diesel-driven ATLANTIC EMPRESS. Ironically, when sold in 1963, she was put under the red ensign as SEA EMPRESS by Vergocean Steamship Co. Ltd., a subsidiary of the Greek Vergottis family. By now simply EMPRESS, she arrived at Shanghai on 5th June 1973 to be broken up.

GEORGIOS
William Gray & Co. Ltd., West Hartlepool; 1951, 7564gt, 457 feet
The more conservative N.G. Livanos ordered steam tramps from Grays, which were little more than refined versions of the war-built B type. These included MARY (5,685/1949) and GEORGIOS, the latter seen here in London when under the Liberian flag. In the 1960s, many Greek-owned ships were reflagged in Greece, and this happened to GEORGIOS in 1965. After a respectable 18 years with N.G. Livanos, in 1969 GEORGIOS was sold to Italian owners who returned her to Liberian registry as MAYROSE. Over the next nine years, she also spent periods as SYMPATHY and UNION AMERICA, as which she arrived at Kaohsiung on 11th April 1977 to be broken up.

LUCY (top)
William Gray & Co. Ltd., West Hartlepool; 1957, 7550gt, 457 feet
Built six years after GEORGIOS, the motor ship LUCY is externally almost identical, distinguished from the steamer only by the lack of the cowl-topped funnel. Old-established Greeks were usually particular about the appearance of their ships, and in this photograph of LUCY she lacks the white hull band that was long a feature of Livanos ships, although other photographs show that she did carry the band at some time.

In 1973 LUCY became the LEONIDAS MICHALOS of N. Michalos & Sons, a company who are said to have given the Livanos family the idea for their funnel, Michalos using a similar design with a letter M rather than L. Michalos sold her in 1979 and, as BLESSING, she lasted another two years before arriving at Visakhapatnam on 30th March 1981 to be demolished.

PEARL CREEK (middle)
William Gray & Co. Ltd., West Hartlepool; 1958, 8,692gt, 478 feet
PEARL CREEK was one of five near-sisters ordered by N.G. Livanos from West Hartlepool in the late 1950s, the others being PEARL STONE (8,143/1956), PEARL SEA (8,240/1957), PEARL BEACH (8,692/1958), and PEARL HAVEN (8,461/1960), whilst four others later came from Doxfords. Owners were the Monrovia Shipping Co. Ltd., and the ships were put under the Liberian flag.

The broadside view of the moored PEARL CREEK shows Livanos' elegant funnel design, and the unusual profile of these motor ships. With their two-storey accommodation amidships, their appearance was not unlike the boilers-on-deck steamers built for Dene Shipping Co. Ltd.

In 1965, the managers listed in *Lloyds Confidential Index* became Pearl Carriers Ltd., perhaps indicating some change in the organisation of N.G. Livanos's shipping empire. In 1974, the PEARL CREEK was renamed LEODAMAS under the Greek flag. In 1978 she was sold to become ZINOVIA, a traditional name used by N. Michalos & Sons, but as so often changing the name or – more probably – the crew brought misfortune. Whilst on passage from Dunkirk to Port Sudan she went aground off Ras Gharib Lighthouse on 24th August 1979. Refloated on 20th September, ZINOVIA was beyond economical repair, and sold via the West German breakers Eckhardt & Co. to Taiwanese breakers. However, the old ship did not give up without a fight. Leaving Port Sudan in tow of SUMI MARU No. 35 (498/1974) for Taiwan her tow broke in bad weather on 26th March 1980 and she drifted aground on Duhrab Island. She was not refloated until October, and needed repairs at Djibouti before she could proceed. In the event, she finished her journey at Gadani Beach in December.

PEARL HAVEN (bottom)
William Gray & Co. Ltd., West Hartlepool; 1960, 8,461gt, 478 feet
PEARL HAVEN, seen here approaching Eastham, traded under this name until 1968, when she was renamed THETIS on being sold to the first of a series of smaller Greek owners who, just as Livanos and others had done in previous generations, were building up fleets by buying second-hand tonnage. In 1973 she passed to Pontikos Shipping Agencies and was renamed EVANGELISMOS. As CHIOS she arrived at Kaohsiung on 4th September 1979 to be broken up, having spent the period from December 1974 to mid-1976 at Las Palmas undergoing repairs.

AGHIOS SPYRIDON
Wm. Doxford and Sons (Shipbuilders) Ltd., Sunderland; 1957, 9921gt, 509 feet
In the 1950s Doxfords were simultaneously building motorships like the Chandris vessels with composite superstructure, and others like AGHIOS SPYRIDON to the then rather antiquated split-superstructure design. The reasons for this have been discussed at length in *Putting the Record straight,* and the most likely conclusion is that some traditionally-minded owners preferred to keep their deck officers as far as possible from their engineers. Certainly, the owners of AGHIOS SPYRIDON fell into the traditional class. Contemporary editions of *Lloyds's Confidential Index* list the owners as Porto Blanco Compania Naviera S.A. of Panama, for whom the agents were Rethymnis & Kulukundis Ltd. of London. R & K are amongst the best-known London Greeks, and the Kulukundis family can claim to have been continuously involved in shipowning since 1835. R & K have been associated with such well-known British companies as Counties Ship Management Ltd. and London & Overseas Freighters Ltd., as well as having important fleets under Greek and convenience flags. However, AGHIOS SPYRIDON does not carry the R & K funnel - black or yellow with white over blue bands carrying a red star. The yellow funnel with blue ball belongs to Minas Rethymnis, his cousin Michael Pneumaticos, and brother-in-law Stathis Yanaghas. This grouping of owners originating from Syra had built several tramps in British yards between the wars, culminating in the Doxford-built KASSOS (5,215/1939), the first motorship ever built for Greek account. KASSOS was the forerunner of a very successful series which included MERCHANT PRINCE (5,229/1939). The series developed in the 1950s with deliveries of the AGHIA MARINA (6,498/1954) and AGHIOS NICOLAOS (9,921/1957) and concluded with the AGHIOS SPYRIDON for the same owner.

AGHIOS SPYRIDON moved to the Compania de Navegacion Golfo Azul S.A. in 1965, but did not change her real ownership until 1975 when sold within Greece and renamed TRINITY. She was broken up in South Korea, arriving at Inchon on 17th April 1979.

DIAMANTIS PATERAS
J. Readhead & Sons Ltd., South Shields; 1955, 6,110gt, 460 feet
No effort was made to disguise the ownership of this steamer, and it is hardly necessary to look at *Lloyds's Confidential Index* to work out that agents were Diamantis Pateras Ltd. of London. By the mid 1950s, Diamantis had almost certainly relinquished management to his son, Panaghis D. Pateras. When only two years old the steamer was renamed KYVERNITIS by Pateras, to free the name for a German-built motor ship. In 1959, when only four years old, she was sold out of the fleet to become the People's Republic of China's HOPING WU SHI SSU, subsequently taking the names XING HUO and HONG QI 130. Under the last of these names, which translates as 'Red Flag No.130', she was deleted from registers in 1982.

With her very short career as DIAMANTIS PATERAS, doubts were entertained that the photograph shows the 1955 Readhead-built ship. However, comparison with photographs of steamers built contemporarily by Readheads for H. Hogarth & Sons Ltd. leaves no doubt she came from the South Shields yard, as they show she is similar in almost all details. A notable difference is that, on the BARON INVERCLYDE (5,479/1954), BARON OGILVY (5,471/1956) and BARON BERWICK (5,471/1956), the superstructure is trunked alongside number 3 hatch. Could the DIAMANTIS PATERAS be an example of an owner insisting on rigid separation of deck officers and engineers?

SHORT'S ELEGANCE

PINDAR

Short Brothers Ltd., Sunderland; 1954, 6,129gt, 491 feet,

The funnel of Lyras Brothers Ltd. was unmistakable and the lyre left no doubt as to the identity of her owner. Sadly, it is quite rare, as the fleet has never been large, and under its current incarnation of Lyras Maritime Ltd., consists of just four vessels. This view of PINDAR shows the funnel well, and also throws in doubt the sometimes perjorative term 'tramp' applied to these ships. With her excellent outfit of cargo gear, including a heavy lift derrick at her foremast, PINDAR could pass for a cargo liner in any company. The stern view also reveals that the photograph was an early one, as in 1957 PINDAR swopped the Liberian registry for Greek. Flags-of-convenience were not invented by the Greeks. Some respectable British owners like Alfred Holt found it expedient to register ships overseas, and various US rum-runners and oil companies have the honour of first using the flags of Panama and Liberia. But Greek owners probably made most profit out of flags-of-convenience. They claimed that they were driven to using them after the Second World War by political instability in Greece (where civil war continued until 1949), by the punitive tax demands of their government, and by militancy amongst Greek seamen's unions. However, whilst not dismissing these factors, Gelina Harlaftis – probably Greece's leading maritime historian – believes that the USA made flags-of-convenience as attractive as possible to Greeks to suit its own ends. The USA strongly supported Panama and Liberia as flags-of-convenience because the many Greek and other ships under these flags gave the USA a low-cost tramp fleet which, during the cold war period, they could easily control. Towards the end of the 1950s, there began a slow drift back to the Greek flag. This was due partly to the Greek Government making Greek registry financially more attractive, a policy which attracted owners as freight rates fell and other maritime powers, such as Britain and Norway, campaigned against flags of convenience.

PINDAR's further career falls into the same pattern as that of the other Greek ships shown here. In 1970 she took the name VASILAKIS without change of ownership, and only after completing almost two decades of work was she sold by Lyras. As UNITY, she worked from 1973 until her arrival at Ulsan, Korea for demolition on 9th March 1979. UNITY was under the same disponent ownership as TRINITY ex AGHIOS SPYRIDON, namely M.P. Tsikopoulos, who operated a large fleet in the 1970s as Navarino Shipping & Transport Co. Ltd. In the photograph, note the US car on hatch number 4.

STAMOS

Short Brothers Ltd., Sunderland; 1956, 8789gt, 491 feet,

D.J. Fafalios, who originated from Chios, had a simple funnel design with his Greek initial in white on a blue band on black basic. For his British-subsidiary, Waverley Overseas Freighters Ltd., the letter 'F' replaced the Greek letter. It is interesting that so many Greek owners had ships under the red ensign, and it may be because, somewhat surprisingly, British pay rates were actually lower than Greek rates until 1956, a time when many Greek owners were enticed back to their country's flag.

The STAMOS has an elegance to match the Fafalios funnel, and although her paintwork is not pristine in the photograph there is evidence that the crew have been at work on it. She is very clearly a development of the PINDAR with subtle differences such as an extra pair of king posts aft, and slight changes to the superstructure. Fafalios had over twenty years' work out of the motorship before selling her in 1978 to a Greek newcomer to shipping. She traded as DIMITRIS P - the P standing for Pavlou - until she arrived at Gadani Beach on 13th May 1983.

Postscript

The unmistakeably British lines of these ships, together with the often poorly-recorded histories of their Greek owners, give them a particular fascination. If there is sufficient interest from our readers, it is a subject to which we shall return.

TOWER & ENSIGN EXPRESS SHIPPING LTD.

Ken Garrett

The beginning

Tower Shipping Ltd. was formed in 1965 by the amalgamation of two well-established freight forwarding and shipping agencies, Macdonald Deadman Ltd. of London and Universal Freight Ltd. of Liverpool. They were shortly joined by R.H. Tennens Ltd. of London. The Chairman of the new company was a Mr. D.H. Deadman who retained control until he retired in 1983. The company name came from the intention to acquire offices in the Tower Buildings in Liverpool but, in the event, the plan changed and the new company offices were located in the Liver Buildings although the name was retained. The company logo – displayed on the funnel, bow badge and house flag – took the form of a white crenellated tower on a blue ground. The bow badge was sometimes embellished with an outer ring. At first the new company carried on with the forwarding and agency activities of its constituent partners. However, an early association with J.F. Embleton and Co. Ltd., brokers on the Baltic Exchange, resulted in some small ships being taken on time charter by Tower. This experience, coupled with their knowledge of the contemporary freight market, lead Tower to investigate the possibility of owning ships themselves. They found that it was possible to obtain 25% investment grants from the Government, and together with many tax advantages, this made the building of ships an attractive proposition.

The first ships

Enquiries were put in hand, both in the United Kingdom and on the continent, for suitable tonnage at the small end of the market. At the time, Clelands Shipbuilding Co. Ltd. of Wallsend was actively marketing their XL400 class of ship. This was based on earlier designs, notably Thomas Watson's LADY SERENA (200/1964) and the smaller FIXITY (199/1966) design developed for F.T. Everard and Sons Ltd. by Fellows and Co. Ltd., the shipbuilders of Great Yarmouth. Everards had a considerable influence in the design although they only took two of the ships; yard number 300, FUTURITY (199/1968) and yard number 304, FORMALITY (199/1968). Quotes of about £75,000 each for these 400-ton-deadweight ships were received from Clelands and other quotes from a Dutch yard for slightly larger 600-tonners. At this time there was still a widespread and conservative belief amongst British owners that the Dutch ships were built down to a price and flimsy in consequence, although they were fully up to classification society standards. This notion possibly influenced the choice, but the major factor was the early delivery promised by Kenneth Craggs, the Chairman of Clelands.

The first pair of ships came into service in August 1968. They were yard number 301, TOWER VENTURE, and yard number 303, TOWER CONQUEST. Two sister vessels, yard number 302, TOWER PRINCESS and yard number 305, TOWER DUCHESS, followed in May and June 1969. In order to keep his delivery promises, Kenneth Craggs was forced to sub-contract a fifth vessel to J.R. Hepworth (Hull) Ltd. of Paull who built the TOWER MARIE as their yard number 107. Although built to the same design and looking very similar to the others, she suffered the disadvantage of being some ten tons short of her designed deadweight.

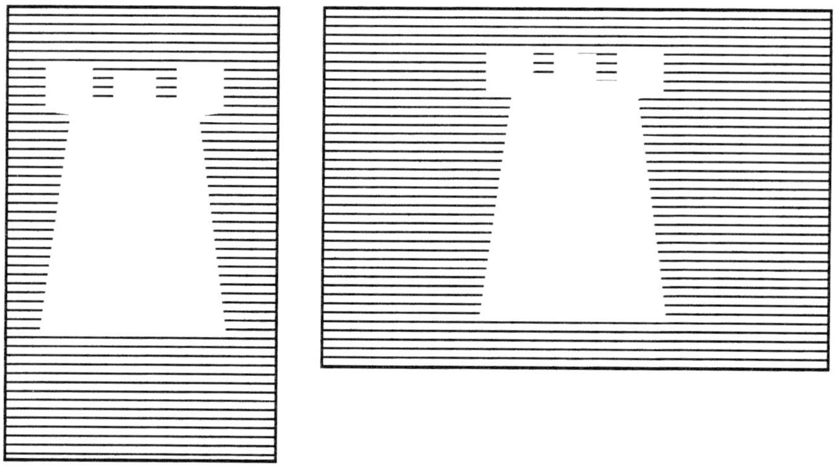

Funnel and flag of Tower Shipping Co. Ltd.: both are light blue (left). *[J.L. Loughran]*

FORMALITY was one of only two XL400 ships delivered to F.T. Everard and Sons Ltd. (opposite top). Sold in 1987 to become EAU DE VIE, she was renamed THAMESWOOD a year later. According to *Lloyd's Register* she has been laid up since October 1996.

TOWER VENTURE (opposite middle). *[CA Hill].*

The containers on board TOWER MARIE emphasise the small size of these coasters (opposite bottom).

ALITY
DON

TOWER VENTURE

TOWER MARIE

TOWER PRINCESS. *[J.K. Byass]*

The choice of names for the first pair is really self evident and the names for the second pair were derived from Mr. Deadman's jocular habit of referring to ladies of his acquaintance as 'princess' or 'duchess'. The fifth ship was named after the wife of one of the directors. The two later Tower ships were named after directors' daughters.

The TOWER PRINCESS caused some excitement in December 1974 when she struck the stern of the gas tanker METHANE PROGRESS (21,875/1964) lying alongside the North Thames Gas Jetty at Canvey Island. She made a three foot hole in the tanker's steering flat and sustained considerable bow damage herself. She was eventually pulled clear, on a rising tide, by the tug SUN XXV (231/1963).

Gross tonnage

An advantage of the small Cleland's ships was the low gross tonnage which, at just below 200 tons, put them beneath the threshold for federated crews and of various international conventions. For example, the requirements of the radio convention started at 300 gross tons and the safety convention at 500 gross tons. The effect of all of this was to eliminate the need for some expensive equipment and surveys but placed the responsibility for an adequate and properly maintained outfit of safety equipment on the owner and the seafarers. The contemporary British manning regulations did not extend to such low tonnages and the original Standards of Training, Certification and Watchkeeping Convention of 1974 left these ships untouched.

Some regulations, falling short of the convention, were made in 1975 following the official enquiry into the FESTIVITY incident. This unfortunate ship was caught in a gale in the North Sea in November 1971 whilst on passage from Rotterdam to Selby with a cargo of soya beans. Her crew abandoned the ship when it appeared to them that it was not answering the helm. She was taken in tow but the towrope parted and she started to drift dangerously close to an oil rig. The tow was reconnected and the ship taken safely into Hull where it was surveyed and no mechanical defects found. The ensuing official enquiry appeared to have some difficulty in reaching any conclusions, but some of the its findings were used by the Government to regulate the operation of small coastal vessels, in particular their manning, training and certification.

Events have moved on with the International Tonnage Convention of 1969 increasing the gross tonnage of these ships. Also the new Standards of Training, Certification and Watchkeeping has caught these ships in its net if they proceed much further than territorial limits. Perhaps more significant is the new International Safety Management Code which, without being prescriptive in terms of inventories of required equipment, does place the responsibility for safe operations, ashore and afloat, fairly and squarely on the owner or operator. Many of the loopholes that made for an economic operation some 30 years ago have been closed and it is doubtful if the revenue potential of such ships is now anywhere near their running costs.

Main engines

With hindsight, the choice of Rolls Royce main DV8MN engines for the early ships did not prove to be particularly wise. The advantages perceived at the time were that the weight was a couple of tons less than an equivalent Kelvin or Lister Blackstone unit and the engine, being shorter than the others, reduced the length of the engine room by two frame spaces, thus providing some extra cargo space. However, much of the saving in weight was absorbed by the skin cooling tanks that were later supplemented by a heat exchanger to cool the main engine. There were also rumours current at the time amongst coastal shipowners concerning the reliability of the cheaper Kelvin engine. But the most powerful inducement was undoubtedly the charisma of the maker's name.

The Dutch-built TOWER HELEN.

In practice, the engines did not perform to expectations and constantly gave trouble, mainly associated with overheating. The exhaust silencer had to be replaced at least every two years and the fuel pumps much more frequently. The engine rooms were very hot and particularly prone to fires: oil splashes were a real hazard if they came into contact with the exhaust system. While on the Isle of Man run in the summer of 1975, the TOWER VENTURE suffered two major engine room fires and had to be towed to safety on each occasion. At the statutory Special Survey or following an engine breakdown, it was quite usual to remove the entire engine and replace it with an exchange unit. The TOWER HELEN had a main engine breakdown at Ostend in January 1975 when the damaged engine was replaced and taken back to the UK for repair in the ship's hold. These exchange units were provided by the engine builders at advantageous rates, no doubt in an endeavour to salvage their reputation. To be fair, the makers probably did not envisage the conditions under which the engines would have to operate or, perhaps, the standards of care and maintenance normally expected on small coastal vessels at that time.

There were frequent discussions about the feasibility of changing the main engines but the cost and difficulties involved and the need to take up some valuable cargo space always overcame the argument for change. In the end, the company learned to live with the problems they could not solve. With all the difficulties, it was, on the face of it, rather surprising when the company opted for a Rolls Royce engine for the first of the Dutch-built ships in 1971. However, the simple truth was that by this time, many of the recurring problems had been overcome by various modifications that could be built into a new ship from the start. Further, the company had built up considerable experience with these engines and also a comprehensive and valuable stock of spare parts.

Trading

For the first year of operation, the ships were operated with assistance from J.F. Embleton and Co. Ltd., the brokers with whom Tower had had a previous association. Thereafter Ted Deadman, who had recently become a director of the company and worked from an office in Stratford in East London, took control of the technical and personnel aspects of the fleet management. The new company had come a long way in a short time and felt well able to look after itself. Trading conditions were good in the early 1970s and operating profits looked healthy, particularly as the ships had been partly financed with government grants. As usual when times are good, it became difficult to keep the ships manned with suitable crews. Many came and went but there was always a nucleus of loyal men some of who stayed with the company throughout its existence. The early, smaller ships had a crew of three or four while the later, larger ships had five or six men. In common with many small, non-federated, coastal vessels the crews were paid on the 'share' system. That is, they received an agreed proportion of the freight revenue earned by the ship, less certain deductions, and the balance was distributed between them according to a negotiated formula.

In general the ships were well occupied trading from the near continent, mainly Rotterdam and Antwerp, to London and other south and east coast ports of the UK. In particular they went to the smaller and usually 'non scheme' ports in the Humber area including New Holland, Selby, Howdendyke, Gunness and Gainsborough. At one time the company had a weekly liner service with general cargo, known as the 'J Line', running from Dreadnought Wharf at Greenwich to Antwerp. A contract to ship china clay from Par in Cornwall to Northfleet on the Thames was won from another well-known London shipowner and such a voyage would be followed with a cargo of bagged cement from Halling, near Rochester to the Channel Islands. With only a short ballast passage back to Par and little in the way of hold cleaning necessary, the two movements made good commercial sense. Although they were not frequent visitors to the west coast, the company had a time charter with Ronagency Shipping Ltd. of the Isle of Man to carry general cargo from Glasson Dock to Castletown. Sometimes this extended to Ireland, running in tandem with a vessel belonging to Hull Gates Shipping Co. Ltd. It was not always the same ship on the time charter but the TOWER VENTURE, DUCHESS or MARIE which were all fitted to carry containers.

On the spot market, one particularly noteworthy cargo was a huge propeller taken from the Birkenhead works of Stone Manganese Marine Ltd. to the Tyne in 1969 for the ESSO NORTHUMBRIA (126,543/1970), a large tanker under construction by Swan Hunter Shipbuilders Ltd. at Wallsend. Carried on deck, the propeller caused some consternation during the passage through the Caledonian Canal because the blade tips overhung the ship's side.

Ships from Holland

With investment grants still available, albeit not quite as generous as in previous years, the company soon cast about for new tonnage. Experience of the original ships had opened their eyes a little wider and the company settled on one of the attractive offers from a Dutch builder. The result was the TOWER HELEN, completed in 1971 and at 645 tons deadweight larger than the earlier British-built ships. She was successful in operation, and well liked by charterers and crews. Tower realised the scale of the opportunity missed in 1968 when they ordered the five smaller ships.

The TOWER HELEN was sold in 1988 and as the BREYDON MERCHANT she briefly hit the national headlines in 1991 when she caught fire on a voyage to Drogheda with a cargo that included explosives. After the fire had been extinguished she was towed into the Thames where her cargo was discharged but the ship was declared a constructive total loss and sold for scrap.

Shortly after the TOWER HELEN was completed, two larger vessels were ordered, again from Dutch builders. They were the TOWER JULIE for Tower Shipping and the FORDONNA for the associated Fordham Navigation Ltd. Both ships were powered by the Mirrlees Blackstone ESL6 Mk2, six-cylinder unit which was very popular at the time but which, within ten years, was eclipsed by more advanced designs from other engine builders.

These two vessels, built with 20% investment grants, were originally planned as 750 tonners. Somehow this was stretched during the building and they ended up at over 900 tons total deadweight and therefore able to carry about 850 tons of cargo. Paradoxically, at that time, 750 tons was the most popular lot size for many coastal bulk cargoes and in these ships' early years the extra tonnage was not necessarily the bonus it had appeared to be. In later years, when the thoughts of shippers went beyond a thousand tons, they had a difficult time again. They were too large for the very smallest berths but not large enough to compete where deep-water berths were involved. They met a setback early in their life when they were declared too wide to pass through the toll bridge at Selby. This prevented them going to Selby and particularly the Olympia Oil and Cake Mill. However, during their mid-life TOWER HELEN and FORDONNA were the most profitable and efficient units of the fleet.

The FORDONNA was the first ship to be managed by Tower Shipping for another owner and she was followed by the NIMROD and SPRING LASS when they were taken into management in the mid 1970s. The NIMROD had the misfortune of being the only ship the company ever lost when she capsized and sank in the North Sea after her cargo of stone chippings shifted on a voyage from Whitstable to Leith.

When the FORDONNA was purchased in 1976 the company reached its zenith with a fleet of eight ships. Thereafter the numbers declined steadily.

TOWER JULIE at St. Helier, Jersey on 8th August 1975. *[David Hocquard]*

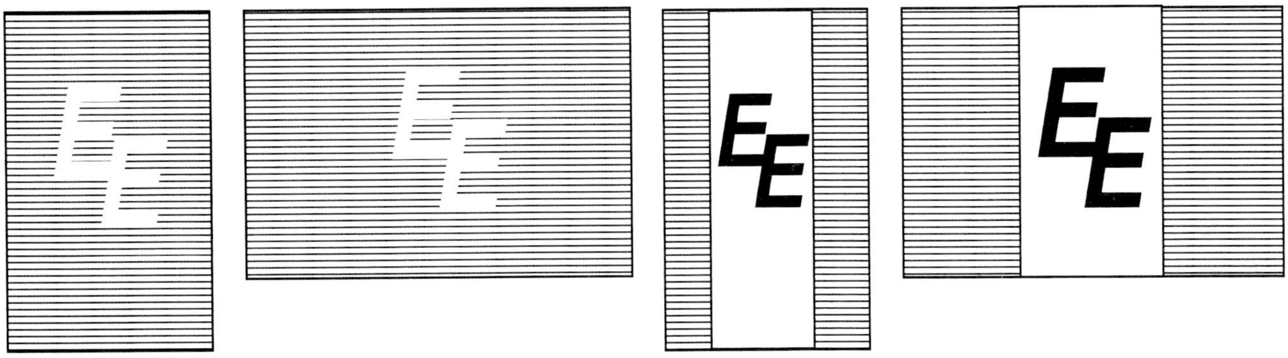

Funnels and flags of Ensign Express Shipping Co. Ltd. The 'official' versions are to the left, but those on the right were reported worn by the ships. The basic colour is light blue. *[J.L. Loughran]*

Ensign Express Shipping Ltd.

By mid 1983 the board of Tower Shipping decided that it no longer wished to be involved in shipowning. Ted Deadman organised what today would be called a management buy-out and gained control of the ships through the medium of a dormant Tower Shipping subsidiary, the Ensign Express Shipping Ltd., which had been in existence since the days of the Antwerp liner service. The company began trading under the new management in December 1983. At that time the fleet consisted of four ships; TOWER DUCHESS, TOWER HELEN, TOWER JULIE and FORDONNA. The 'double E' funnel mark and houseflag was the result of a desk doodle by the new owner.

The TOWER DUCHESS, the last remaining ship of the original quartet from Clelands was soon sold. Whatever their faults, the rugged nature of these little ships, now 30 years old, can be seen by their subsequent careers with two going to Newfoundland to face an extreme and hostile environment while another has been spotted enjoying the warmer climes of Mauritius.

Later trades

With an eye on the lucrative ammonium nitrate trade from Sluiskil on the Ghent Canal to various ports on the east coast of the UK, Ensign Express negotiated the purchase of the RIVER DART from General Freight Ltd., one of the Unilever group companics. The sale was prompted by a decision of the Unilever board to sell all its transport elements whether by land or sea. The transaction took place in July 1985 and the directors of General Freight entertained Ted Deadman to lunch to mark the occasion of the sale of their last remaining ship.

The ship, previously managed by F.T. Everard & Sons Ltd., was engaged on a time charter to Genchart of Amsterdam to carry steel from the Hoogevan Estel works at Ijmuiden to various small British ports including Howdendyke and Whitby. This business was good and the time charter was maintained by the new owner. Meanwhile, the TOWER JULIE and the FORDONNA had portable bulkheads fitted in their holds to provide the necessary space between the engine room and the ammonium nitrate cargo. This fertilizer is classified in the International Dangerous

RIVER DART. *[Fotoflite incorporating Skyfotos]*

Goods Code as a Class 5.1 oxidising substance and has to be treated with great care. The ships were engaged on consecutive voyages for a lengthy period on annual contracts of affreightment but Nederlandse Stikstof Maatschappij B.V. (N.S.M.) did not offer any time charters. A number of other coastal owners including Everards, Wilks, and Crescent were involved in the trade from Sluiskil across the North Sea to the Humber and also further afield to various French ports. The work came to an abrupt end when the new fertilizer plant came into production at Immingham and was able to satisfy the British market. To complete the international picture, both the British and Dutch fertilizer plants are now part of the Norske Hydro group.

Running down

By 1988 the fleet was reduced to three vessels, TOWER JULIE, FORDONNA and RIVER DART. The fertilizer work had come to an end and the steel charter had been taken by Crescent Shipping. Ships from other British companies also lost their steel charters when the specially built STEEL SPRINTER (993/1985) and STEEL SHUTTLE (993/1985) came into service. This core business was almost impossible to replace on the open spot market with anything like an adequate return. The struggle became even harder as the recession bit still deeper; and when earnings were consistently less than the fuel, wages and other disbursements there was no alternative but to lay up and wait for better times or for a sale. The ships were kept carefully in a state of readiness to take the opportunity of a good paying cargo. With the exception of the RIVER DART this did not happen very often and the two larger ships remained tied up at Goole for lengthy periods.

Postscript

Attempts were made to sell the company in 1990 but no acceptable offer was made and eventually the TOWER JULIE and FORDONNA were sold separately. The company office, which had been in Ramsgate since moving from London in 1987, was closed and the management of the sole remaining vessel, RIVER DART, was entrusted to G.T. Gillie & Blair Ltd. of Newcastle-upon-Tyne.

It is fruitless, yet interesting, to speculate on what might have been. When the office at Ramsgate was closed, some correspondence and quotations were discovered relating to proposed 650 ton ships from Dutch builders at the time the original Clelands ships were built. Would these larger ships with more reliable engines have given the company a firmer foundation by taking greater advantage of the good trading conditions of the early 1970s? Or perhaps the larger ships might have hastened the demise when the recession hit coastal shipping. Whatever the result, the company could not have been run with more dedication: it remained with the British flag, employed British seafarers and honoured its commitments to training unlike many other coastal and deep-sea fleets. Perhaps typical of a number of companies that started in the heady days of the 1960s and 1970s, Tower and its successor, Ensign Express, have shown a longevity greater than average.

Once again the RIVER DART has taken her place in history. A bonny little ship, she really does not deserve her fate. She was the last coaster in General Freight ownership and now she is the last ship owned by Ensign Express. It is premature to write off the company but at the same time it will be interesting to see if history repeats itself or whether it will be third time lucky for some future owner of RIVER DART.

Fleet list

1. **TOWER VENTURE** 1968-1980
O.N. 335883 200g 162n 435d 41.89 x 7.73 x 2.70 metres
8-cyl. 4SA V oil engine made by Rolls-Royce Motors Ltd., Shrewsbury.
8.7.1968: Launched by Clelands Shipbuilding Co. Ltd., Wallsend (Yard No. 301) for Tower Shipping Ltd., London as TOWER VENTURE.
8.1968: Completed.
1980: Sold to T.J., A.H. and G.J. Palmer, Gravesend and B.F. and R.A. Sully, Norwich and renamed SUBRO VEGA.
1986: Sold to Sully Freight (G.F. Sully Ltd., managers), Norwich.
1989: Sold to Claymorr Shipping Ltd., St. Johns, Newfoundland and renamed CLAYMORR TRANSPORT.
1994: Sold to Blue Star International Trading Inc., Belize and renamed ESMERELDAS EXPRESS.
22.12.1994: Sank in approximate position 07.01 north 79.28 west after taking a list soon after sailing from Esmereldas.

2. **TOWER CONQUEST** 1968-1979
O.N. 335910 200g 162n 430d 41.89 x 7.73 x 2.70 metres
8-cyl. 4SA V oil engine made by Rolls-Royce Motors Ltd., Shrewsbury.
25.7.1968: Launched by Clelands Shipbuilding Co. Ltd., Wallsend (Yard No. 303) for Tower Shipping Ltd., London as TOWER CONQUEST.
8.1968: Completed.
1979: Sold to Adriana B.V. (Visser & Visser Chartering B.V., managers), Rotterdam, Holland and renamed ELST.
1980: Sold to Siebe Elsinga, Panama and renamed GIENY S.
6.1983: Re-engined with a 6-cyl. 4SA oil engine made by Cummins Engine Co. Inc., Columbus, Indiana, USA.
1984: Sold to Medway Coasters Ltd., Rochester.
1989: Sold to J. de Roche and A. Roberts, Grenada.
1995: Used as a storage hulk at St. Georges Harbour, Grenada and later expended for use in landfill operations.

3. **TOWER PRINCESS** 1969-1981
O.N. 337199 200g 161n 430d 41.86 x 7.73 x 2.70 metres
8-cyl. 4SA V oil engine made by Rolls-Royce Motors Ltd., Shrewsbury.
3.4.1969: Launched by Clelands Shipbuilding Co. Ltd., Wallsend (Yard No. 302) for Tower Shipping Ltd., London as TOWER PRINCESS.
5.1969: Completed.
1981: Sold to Matthew Ship Chartering Ltd., Georgetown, Cayman Islands and renamed BRAC EXPRESS.
1984: Owner became Matthew Shipping Co. (Cayman) Ltd., Georgetown, Cayman Islands.
1989: Sold to Naviera Brac Express S. de R.L., San Lorenzo, Honduras and renamed G. & S. EXPRESS.
12.5.1990: Foundered off the north coast of Cuba while on passage from Miami to Haiti with a general cargo.

4. **TOWER DUCHESS** 1969-1984
O.N. 337849 200g 161n 430d 41.86 x 7.73 x 2.70 metres
8-cyl. 4SA V oil engine made by Rolls-Royce Motors Ltd., Shrewsbury.
31.5.1969: Launched by Clelands Shipbuilding Co. Ltd.,

TOWER CONQUEST. *[Fotoflite incorporating Skyfotos]*

Wallsend (Yard No. 305) for Tower Shipping Ltd., London as TOWER DUCHESS.
6.1969: Completed.
12.1983: Acquired by Ensign Express Shipping Ltd., London.
3.1984: Sold to R.B. Berkshire, St. Johns, Newfoundland and renamed PARADISE SOUND.
Continued existence doubtful (1998).

5. **TOWER MARIE** 1969-1980.
O.N. 338010 199g 149n 424d 41.84 x 7.73 x 2.69 metres
8-cyl. 4SA V oil engine made by Rolls-Royce Motors Ltd., Shrewsbury.
15.9.1969: Launched by J.R. Hepworth (Hull) Ltd., Paull (Yard No. 107) for Tower Shipping Ltd., London as TOWER MARIE.
10.1969: Completed.
1980: Sold to Sully Freight, Norwich and renamed SUBRO VIXEN.
1986: Sold to Mezeron Ltd., Ramsey, Isle of Man and renamed COLBY RIVER.
1991: Sold to Northwood (Fareham) Ltd., Fareham and renamed MEDINA RIVER.
Laid up at Fareham (1998).

6. **TOWER HELEN** 1971-1988.
O.N. 341309 425g 262n 645d 47.76 x 8.82 x 3.12 metres
8-cyl. 4SA V oil engine made by Rolls-Royce Motors Ltd., Shrewsbury.
5.1971: Completed by Scheepswerf Ton Bodewes N.V., Franeker, Holland (Yard No. F 44) for Tower Shipping Ltd., London as TOWER HELEN.
12.1983: Acquired by Ensign Express Shipping Ltd., London.
9.1988: Sold to Breydon Marine Ltd., Great Yarmouth and renamed BREYDON MERCHANT.
24.2.1991: Abandoned by her crew after fire had broken out in the accommodation in position 50.38 north 00.30

TOWER DUCHESS. *[C.A. Hill]*

FORDONNA. *[C.A. Hill]*

west during a voyage from Great Oakley to Drogheda with a cargo that included explosives. Taken in tow by the British tug AVENGER (299/1975) and arrived at the Sunk Anchorage on 26.2.1991. The cargo was subsequently discharged and the vessel declared a constructive total loss. She was sold to Masterman Iron & Steel Ship-breakers Ltd., for demolition at Bloors Wharf, Rainham where she arrived 18.6.1991.

7. **TOWER JULIE** 1972-1990
O.N. 343108 499g 323n 920d 55.81 x 9.94 x 3.25 metres
6-cyl 4SA oil engine made by Mirrlees Blackstone Ltd., Stamford.
27.1.1972: Launched by Scheepswerf G. Bijlsma & Zonen N.V., Wartena, Holland (Yard No 588) for Tower Shipping Ltd., London as TOWER JULIE.
3.1972: Completed.
12.1983: Acquired by Ensign Express Shipping Ltd., London.
12.1990: Sold to Gronqvist & Gronqvist Kb., Porvoo/Borga, Finland.
1994: Tonnages (ITC'69) became 572g and 310n.
Still in service (1998).

8. **FORDONNA** 1976-1991
O.N. 358767 499g 323n 905d 55.81 x 9.94 x 3.23 metres
6-cyl. 4SA oil engine made by Mirrlees Blackstone Ltd., Stamford.
11.1972: Launched by Bodewes Scheepswerf 'Volharding' N.V., Foxhol, Holland (Yard No. 172) for Fordham Navigation Ltd., Sark, Channel Islands (Tower Shipping Ltd., London, managers) as FORDONNA.
12.1972: Completed.
1976: Acquired by Tower Shipping Ltd., London.
12.1983: Acquired by Ensign Express Ltd., London.
5.1991: Sold to Nimrod Shipping Ltd., Hamilton, Bermuda (Genchem Ltd., Ipswich, managers).
1994: Sold to Worthtake Ltd., same managers.
Tonnages (ITC'69) became 557g. 301n.
5.1995: Sold to Salcus Shipping Ltd., Belize, (Baltway Shipping Ltd., Kaliningrad, Russia, managers) and renamed DONNA.
Still in service (1998).

9. **RIVER DART** 1985-
O.N. 391006 499g 348n 825d 50.02 x 9.28 x 3.36 metres
5-cyl 4SA oil engine made by Aabenraa Motorfabrik, H.Callesen A/S, Aabenraa, Denmark.
6.1981: Completed by A/S Nordsovaerftet, Ringkobing, Denmark (Yard No. 148) for General Freight Co. Ltd., (F.T. Everard & Sons Ltd., managers), London as RIVER DART.
7.1985: Acquired by Ensign Express Shipping Ltd., London.
1991: G.T. Gillie & Blair Ltd., Newcastle-upon-Tyne ,appointed managers.
1994: Tonnages (ITC'69) became 536g. 262n.
6.1995: Firth Shipping Co. Ltd., Newcastle-upon-Tyne, appointed managers.
Still in service (1998).

Managed vessels

M1. **FORDONNA** 1972-1976
See ship no. 8.

M2. **NIMROD** 1973-1977.
O.N. 340519 378g 258n 510d 49.51 x 8.21 x 3.12 metres
6-cyl 4SA oil engine made by Motorenfabriek 'De Industrie', Alphen aan de Rijn, Holland.
30.8.1948: Launched by N.V. Scheepswerf Westerbroek v/h J.G. Broërken, Westerbroek, Holland (Yard No. 129) for D. Schothorst & W. Schuitema (Carebeka N.V., managers), Groningen, Holland as NIMROD.
7.12.1948: Completed.
2.1971: Sold to Wilson & Ison Shipping Co. Ltd., St. Helier, Jersey, Channel Islands.
1973: Nimrod Line Ltd., Newport, Isle of Wight appointed managers.
1973: Sold to Forumcastle Ltd., Westcliff-on-Sea (Tower Shipping Ltd., London, managers).
14.11.1977: Capsized and sank off the Norfolk coast, west of the Dudgeon Light Vessel in position 53.14 north by 01.11 east whilst on passage from Whitstable to Leith with a cargo of stone chippings. Her crew was rescued by the Dutch motor tanker DUTCH MATE (649/1965) and the British motorship NORWAVE (3,540/1965) and landed at Gorleston.

The ill-fated NIMROD, lost in 1977. *[J.K. Byass]*

M3. **SPRING LASS** 1974-1976.
O.N. 362250 432g 255n 680d 55.35x 9.07 x 3.30 metres
6-cyl. 4SA oil engine made by Motorenwerke Mannheim A.G. (M.W.M.), Mannheim, Germany.
2.1966: Launched by Ruhrorter Schiffswerft & Maschinenfabrik G.m.b.H., Duisburg, Germany (Yard No. 362) for Josef Schoning, Harem/Ems, Germany as JO.
1969: Sold to Uwe Heinz Pauls, Bremen, Germany and renamed ORDING.
8.1974: Sold to Springfield Haulage Co. (Hull) Ltd., Hull and renamed SPRING LASS.
8.1974: Sold to Luxchime Co. Ltd., Hull.
12.1974: Acquired by Sasha Shipping Co. Ltd., Hull (Tower Shipping Ltd., London, managers).
10.1976: Sold to Celsius Importers Ltd., Rochester.
1980: Sold to Floydworth Ltd. (Arcom Shipping Management Ltd., managers), Rochester.
1981: Sold to Warrior Shipping Inc. (Marico Shipping Inc., managers), Panama.
26.3.1983: Foundered off Ancona in position 43.08 north by 14.10 east after taking a list in heavy weather on a voyage from Pesaro.

SPRING LASS. *[C.A. Hill]*

OMEGA – THE LAST OF HER RACE

John Naylon

When in 1898 her new German owners gave the name OMEGA – the last letter of the Greek alphabet – to the ex-British four-masted barque DRUMCLIFF, they were showing remarkable prescience, for the OMEGA was to be the world's last cargo-carrying, non-auxiliary, square-rigged, deep-water sailing ship in commercial operation.

Gillison & Chadwick's 'Drum Line'

The DRUMCLIFF began life as a unit of the fleet of James Gillison and Joseph Chadwick, with premises in Mersey Chambers, Liverpool, later moving to Tower Buildings North, Water Street in that city. Gillison & Chadwick initially owned a mixed bag of vessels comprising the elderly iron barques BRITISH ARMY, BRITISH SOVEREIGN and TYTHONUS, and the New Brunswick-built wooden full-rigger CALLIXENE, but from the mid-1870s they began building up a respectable fleet of eight iron vessels, each with the prefix DRUM. The full-riggers DRUMLANRIG (1876) and DRUMPARK (1877) were followed by the fine four-masted ship DRUMBURTON in 1881. Then came a series of four-masted barques, steadily increasing in tonnage: the DRUMMUIR (1882), the sister ships DRUMBLAIR and DRUMELTAN (1883), the DRUMCRAIG (1885) and the DRUMCLIFF (1887). The ninth and final 'Drum' was the huge steel four-masted barque DRUMROCK of 1891, an awe-inspiring three skysail-yarder and one of the finest sailing ships built in the United Kingdom. She was fitted with a complete hospital under the poop and baths for all hands – an unheard-of luxury aboard a windjammer. The DRUMROCK could lift around 5,000 tons of grain and was commanded by Captain T.S. Bailey during her British career.

Gillison & Chadwick were active in the colonial emigrant trade in the 1870s and '80s, the DRUMMUIR, for example, taking 52 emigrants to Melbourne on her maiden voyage from Liverpool, and the tiny TYTHONUS carrying no less than 103 passengers out to Auckland, New Zealand from London in 1882-3. Their vessels also sailed to India in their early days, but as time went by gradually drifted into the humdrum Pacific and Antipodean grain, nitrate and lumber trades.

With the depression in freight rates and increasing foreign competition at the turn of the century, Gillison & Chadwick began to sell off their sailing vessels to Germany, Italy, Norway, British Columbia and even China. The last to go were the DRUMCRAIG in 1902 and the DRUMBLAIR in 1905. The company had already begun in 1890 to purchase modest-sized, mostly Sunderland-built steel screw steamers of 2-3,000 tons, retaining the prefix DRUM but changing its style to The Astral Shipping Co. Ltd. (Gillison & Chadwick, managers). From four vessels in 1900 the steam fleet increased to seven by 1907, with more modern units and the firm

The DRUMCLIFF at San Francisco in her Gillison and Chadwick livery of grey hull with a broad black bulwark stripe. Her yards squared to a T, she carries the 'Liverpool' or 'English' rig of her time, with single topgallants, as opposed to the 'Scottish' rig of double topgallants. A new ship, the canvas on her boarding ladder proudly displays her name. *[Wilhelm Hester collection, San Francisco Maritime National Park]*

now known as Joseph Chadwick & Son (Astral Shipping Co. Ltd.) of 5 Rumford Place, Liverpool. However, by the end of the First World War, in 1919, the company (now of 601 Tower Buildings, Liverpool) was only operating the 4,921-ton steel screw steamer KANDY (the former German MOLTKEFELS, built at Flensburg in 1904 and a war-reparations acquisition) and the tradition of the 'Drums' had gone.

The DRUMCLIFF

The DRUMCLIFF was launched in January 1887 by Russell & Co. of Greenock. She was reputed to have been built as a four-masted full-rigger, as were the DRUMBLAIR, DRUMELTAN and DRUMMUIR, but photographs of these vessels show their jigger masts as always those of barques. It was not uncommon for *Lloyd's Registers* of that time to record four-masted barques as ships. Winston Langdon, writing in *Log Chips*, July 1953, suggests that up to the 1890s Lloyds' surveyors reported as a 'ship' any vessel fitted with a top (rather than crosstrees) on the after mast, regardless of whether square yards were crossed. If true, this would explain the large number of four-masted barques said to have been launched as ships, and the numerous vessels apparently converted from four-masted ship to four-masted barque rig around 1890.

At 2,525 tons gross and 2,468 tons net, on dimensions 311.3 x 43.2 x 24.2 feet, the DRUMCLIFF was the biggest vessel in the fleet until the DRUMROCK came out in 1891. She was a good 500 tons larger than the DRUMCRAIG, built two years earlier, but 657 tons smaller than the DRUMROCK. Like most of the 'Drums' except the speedy DRUMBURTON she was designed to be a good carrier.

The DRUMCLIFF spent eleven years under the British flag, mostly under the command of Captain H. Davies. A well-maintained vessel, she sailed with a crew of no less than 42 in her prime. Among her apprentices who afterwards became well-known was Captain Luke Ward, marine superintendent of the Cunard Line. No doubt she was regarded as a desirable purchase when Gillison & Chadwick began to break up their sailing fleet and she went to new Hamburg owners in 1898.

The Rhederei-Aktien-Gesellschaft von 1896

Although it had only been founded two years previously by the shipbrokers Axel and Willy Dahlström, the '1896 Company', as it was widely known, was already on its way to becoming the largest sailing-ship owner in Germany. The fleet was rapidly built up by purchases of second- and even third-hand German and English tonnage, the only vessel bought directly from the builders being the bald-headed full-rigger OLINDA (later the British CARDINIA), launched by A. Rodger & Co. at Port Glasgow in 1903.

The iron hulls of the 1870s and 1880s probably represented the peak of elegance of sailing-ship design. The clean profile of the OMEGA shows to advantage in this photograph taken at Port Adelaide, South Australia in 1898-9 during her first voyage for the 1896 Company. She had come out from the Lizard in 81 days under Captain Krause. The small half-round midship house is much less obtrusive than the bigger straight-sided structures of later vessels – notably the Laiesz Flying-P ships – which were very prominent and gave the hull a heavy 'three-island' look. In the OMEGA the midship house does not interrupt the line of the sheer from the half-round poop, the neatest style of stern ever fitted to iron and steel sailing vessels, to the bow. The bowsprit sits on top of the forecastle head, which itself is very little elevated above the main rail, thus allowing the sheer to continue smoothly up to the figurehead. That these aesthetics counted with the shipbuilders of the day is borne out by the comment on midship houses in Thomas H. Watson's *Naval Architecture: A Manual on Laying-Off Iron, Steel and Composite Vessels* (Longman, Green and Co., London): 'To prevent these erections from giving a heavy appearance to the vessel, they are usually moulded away at the sides above the main rail'. After coming under German ownership the OMEGA carried only a small leg-of-mutton spanker, presumably to correct a tendency to gripe. *[Maritime Museum of Monterey].*

The firm started business with the first-class 1,554 gt iron clipper MAULESDEN, built in 1875 by Stephen & Sons of Dundee for David Bruce's Dundee Clipper Line and renamed ORTRUD. The DRUMCLIFF, prophetically renamed OMEGA, was the fifth unit to join the fleet. Up to 1906 the company remained small and indeed did not pay a dividend between 1902 and 1905; but in 1906 the nitrate trade picked up and in that year the 1896 Company took over the entire fleet of B. Wencke Söhne of Hamburg when the latter was wound up on the death of Friedrich Wencke. On the basis of a huge bank loan, 16 vessels – nine full-riggers and seven four-masted barques – were suddenly acquired, together with their captains and crews, thus creating a fleet of 20 ships totalling 41,546 gross tons. Beginning with the ORTRUD the 1896 Company's ships' names began with the letter O, while those taken over from Wencke were derived from Greek mythology (ATHENE, HEBE, HERA, etc.). The policy of take-over continued: in 1907 two more sailers were acquired from the Reederei N.H.P. Schuldt and in 1913 two full-riggers and four four-masted barques from D.H. Wätjen & Co. of Bremen. Altogether 42 vessels passed through the 1896 Company's hands. At the outbreak of the First World War it owned 22 sailing ships totalling 51,500 gross tons (compared with the 14 vessels of Laeisz' better-known Flying P Line) and thus was Germany's biggest sailing-ship company.

The OMEGA under the German flag

The OMEGA served her Hamburg owners for 16 years under Captains Krause, Ratzsch, Schellhass, Oellrich, Hammer and Niejahr. She was engaged in the usual latter-day windjammer trades – general cargo from Hamburg to Pacific or Australian ports, coke to Mexico, coal from Newcastle, NSW to the West Coast of South America, Chilean nitrate, Puget Sound lumber and San Francisco grain to Europe – and made some smart passages. In 1898-9, on her first voyage under the German flag, commanded by Captain Krause, she went from the Lizard to Port Adelaide in 86 days, and then from Newcastle, New South Wales to Tocopilla in 41 days; and in 1906 she reached the Lizard from Port Townsend in 114 days under Captain Ratzsch.

On 21st December 1910 the OMEGA sailed from Portland, Oregon, under Captain Oellrich, with a very special cargo of timber for Hamburg, which she reached in the good time of 120 days. This was 1,850,952 feet of selected and seasoned Oregon fir, valued at $62,310.44 and said to be the most costly timber cargo ever dispatched from Portland. It was to be the decking for the new Hamburg-Amerika trans-Atlantic passenger liner EUROPA, then being built by Blohm & Voss at Hamburg and intended to be the world's largest vessel. The EUROPA subsequently became the VATERLAND, then in 1917 the United States transport LEVIATHAN, and finally a luxury liner for United States Lines 1923-34.

War and internment

The First World War proved catastrophic for the 1896 Company (which in 1913 had declared a good dividend of 12 per cent) and for the German sail fleet in general. At the outset of the war Germany still possessed approximately 140 deep-water square-riggers, mainly hailing from Hamburg and Bremen. No less than 136 of these were seized at sea or

The OMEGA leaving San Diego, California in 1910, in two photographs taken by Lee Passmore (left and opposite top). The OMEGA had come out to San Diego in 159 days from Newcastle-upon-Tyne, under Captain Oellrich. She went on to Portland, Oregon in ballast in 29 days and then, carrying a special timber cargo for the decking of the new trans-Atlantic liner EUROPA, made an excellent homeward passage of 116 days to the Channel and 120 days to Hamburg. In the bow view the timber-loading port is clearly visible in the bow plating.

Opposite bottom: the OMEGA at Callao on 8th April 1917, still looking spruce after two-and-a-half years' internment. Sails have been sent down for the duration of the war and an awning has been spread over the spanker boom to shade the poop from the Peruvian sun. The reason for the flag display is not known – perhaps Captain Niejahr's birthday? Under the 1896 Company's ownership the OMEGA was initially painted black, and later an attractive light grey with a narrow blue stripe. In the background, Wachsmuth and Krogmann's barque TELLUS also lies interned. *[All: Jùrgen Meyer collection]*

interned in foreign ports, to be subsequently handed over to the victorious Allies. The largest single firm to suffer was the 1896 Company, which lost 22 ships; Laeisz lost 18 vessels and Knohr & Burchard 17, so that Hamburg owners were particularly hard hit. During the war eight of the 1896 Company's vessels were seized by the Allies and two were sold to Norway, and in 1919 the remaining 12 sailers were allocated to France, Italy, Finland and Peru. The company re-established itself between 1921 and 1927, but with steamships, although these were named in honour of the sailing ships they replaced.

When the war broke out in August 1914 nearly half the fleet of German sailing ships was on the West Coast of South America or on their way there; in most cases their crews did not learn the news until they arrived at their destinations. Fifty-eight vessels were caught by the war and interned in Chilean ports, four in Peru and 12 in Santa Rosalía, Mexico. For six years they gradually deteriorated, their crews deserting and their inactivity eating away at their owners' finances.

In the case of the OMEGA, Captain Niejahr brought a cargo of wheat from Oregon to the UK early in 1914 and then went out to Callao to load nitrate, only to remain interned there for the duration of the war.

Peruvian cadet ship

In 1919 the vessel was awarded to Peru as a prize, together with her stable-mates the full-rigger MAIPO and the four-masted barque HEBE, and Wachsmuth & Krogmann's barque TELLUS, and became a cargo-carrying cadet ship for the Peruvian government.

Chilean nitrate was still in demand in Europe and freight rates remained high for 18 months after the Armistice. A group of German shipowners whose vessels were scattered along the Chilean coast formed the German Sailing Ship Office in Hamburg and, by arrangement with the Allied Reparations Commission in London, sent out the Woermann steamer LUCIE WOERMANN with several hundred seamen to bring their ships back home. In 1920 47 German windjammers which had been interned in the nitrate ports were sailed to Europe by disaffected and disorderly crews, and 45 of them were immediately handed over to the UK, France, Italy and Greece. The following year a great fleet of 61 square-riggers brought nitrate to Europe, the last year of such sailing-ship activity. Many of these vessels (and of the 68 square-riggers which loaded Australian grain that year) would never make another commercial voyage, due to slump setting in.

The OMEGA formed part of the 1921 fleet, bringing nitrate to London and returning to Callao from Barry in the poor time of 132 days. Although flying the Peruvian flag she was commanded and officered by Germans, some of whom had married in Peru during the war and had acquired Peruvian citizenship.

A 1925 ocean 'race'

In 1924-5 the OMEGA made a second and last protracted voyage to Europe and back, after which she never rounded Cape Horn again. Following a very slow passage from Callao to Dublin she crossed over to the Mersey but could not obtain a return freight. Accordingly she left the Mersey for Callao in ballast on Monday, 16th February 1925 in tow of Rea's tug POOLGARTH. She had already made two attempts to get out of the Irish Sea south-about, via the Tuskar, and now decided to try north-about via Rathlin Island. This third effort to leave her original home waters was equally fraught. A strong northerly wind forced tug and tow to anchor in Ramsey Bay, Isle of Man, on Wednesday, 18th February; on the Thursday, with the wind still northerly, they set off south once more; and only on Friday, 20th February was the OMEGA finally able to cast off from the POOLGARTH south of the Tuskar – which is when some of the photographs accompanying this article were taken by Cooper of Seacombe.

Two other German square-riggers left England for Callao at the same time as the OMEGA, the barque OBOTRITA sailing from the Mersey on 16th February, the same day as the OMEGA, and the full-rigger GREIF leaving Plymouth the previous day. All three were in ballast but the outcome of the 'race' could not have been more contrasted. The little OBOTRITA arrived in Callao in the fast time of 81 days – well up to the standards of the German nitrate clippers – whereas the other two ships took 143 days (GREIF) and 144 (OMEGA). The GREIF was quoted at 20 guineas on the re-insurance market before she arrived, while the OMEGA lost her rudder in heavy weather in the South Atlantic and completed the passage with a jury rudder.

Neither the OBOTRITA nor the GREIF was to last much longer after going out to Callao with the OMEGA. After her 81-day passage in 1925 the OBOTRITA – which had been a stable-mate of the OMEGA under the 1896 Company's flag between 1902 and 1911 – loaded guano at Pachacamac for Terneuzen but stranded on the Belgian coast between Blankenberghe and Ostende on the night of 25-26th November 1925. Although she was got off she was broken up at Dordrecht in 1926. The GREIF (originally Windram's WISCOMBE PARK) went aground on the Twin Rocks outside Belfast on 10th June 1927 after a rough passage of 126 days from Port Pirie to Falmouth with grain. Again, although she was salvaged and towed to Belfast, as soon as her cargo was out she went to the scrappers for £2,500. The OMEGA was to outlive the OBOTRITA and GREIF by another 30 years.

The Peruvian guano fleet

After her protracted passage from the Mersey to Callao in 1925 the OMEGA was laid up for a while and then in 1926 passed into the hands of the Compañía Administradora del Guano, with headquarters in Lima and home port Callao. For the rest of her life the OMEGA remained on the Peruvian coast. The vessels of the government guano monopoly loaded at the Chinchas and other islands lying a couple of hundred miles offshore, such as the Santa Rosa Islands 150 miles south of Callao, and delivered their cargoes at small ports along the mainland for distribution to the sugar plantations inland. For over three decades after the Great War the Compañía Administradora del Guano ran a little anachronistic fleet of three square-riggers which intrigued and delighted sail enthusiasts – the OMEGA, MAIPO and TELLUS, all Germans which had been stranded at Callao 1914-18 and had been taken over by the Peruvian government.

The 1,770gt full-rigger MAIPO had been built in 1893 by Tecklenborg of Geestemunde for N.H.P. Schuldt of Hamburg and had passed to the 1896 Company in 1907. She had a good turn of speed, going from Newcastle, NSW to Caldera in 36 days in 1912, under Captain G. Ahlers. The 1,468gt barque TELLUS was originally the Dutch EVERTSEN, built by Rijkee & Co. of Rotterdam in 1891, and had been owned by Wachsmuth & Krogmann of Hamburg since 1907.

The last days of sail on the West Coast

All three relics of the past continued to work until well into the 1950s, sailing northward from the guano islands and occasionally towing south against the Peruvian current. They steadily deteriorated in condition; with patched canvas, worn and rotten rigging, and unpainted barnacle-encrusted hulls, they were in no shape for heavy-weather sailing. The

Friday, 20th February 1925, south of the Tuskar. After five days beating about in the Irish Sea the OMEGA is finally able to let go of her tug and set sail for Callao, leaving European waters for the last time. She is once more painted a utilitarian black. The fore and mizzen royal yards have been sent down for the ballast passage and no sail is bent on the main royal yard. In the lower picture two men can be seen on the main yard, slacking off the buntlines as the mainsail is set. H.N. Cooper who took the photographs from Rea's tug POOLGARTH, published the 'Anchor' series of sailing-ship photographs between the wars.

OMEGA's royal yards were removed and the topgallants were no longer used for fear the spars, masts and rigging would not take the strain. Only the TELLUS had a complete set of sails.

In 1951 the OMEGA stranded in shallow water off San Lorenzo, the large island which guards the approaches to Callao, while en route to Puerto Chicama with guano; but she was got off with only minor damage, her plates and rigging were renewed in the naval dockyard, and she was sent back into service. The TELLUS and MAIPO were laid up in 1953 but the OMEGA was again dry-docked and refitted in 1954. In that same year all three were reported for sale at Callao with an asking price of $25,000 each, but there were no takers. The San Francisco Maritime Museum was said to have offered $10,000 for any one of the trio, delivered in San Francisco, but the offer was turned down because the cost of towing would be prohibitive.

In 1956 all three were put up for auction no less than nine times, with the reserve price gradually reducing from $30,000 to $12,000, but there were still no bids, and the MAIPO was broken up at Callao. The TELLUS, which in 1954 had briefly been renamed MALABOO and converted into a floating yacht clubhouse – which failed – left Callao on 23rd May 1957 in tow of the Portuguese tug PRAIA GRANDE, loaded with 2,000 tons of scrap iron, and was taken via the Panama Canal to Belgium for scrapping.

The last survivor

Only the OMEGA lingered on, commanded in her latter years by Captain Erik Hanke, a German who had become a naturalized Peruvian and who was about the same age as his ship. Captain Hanke had first joined the OMEGA in 1924 as second mate, at the commencement of her second post-war voyage to Europe, and then, after serving in steam, had gone back to her in the 1950s when facing retirement. The only other officer was the chief mate, a Peruvian of similar age. The sailmaker, who in 1953 was aged 80, was a Quechua Indian who had also joined the vessel as ordinary seaman in 1924. Besides these, only the steward and bosun were veteran seamen, the remainder being young scratch crews.

Finally, on 26th June 1958, when Captain Hanke was on leave and the vessel was commanded by her mate, the OMEGA went onto the rocks off San Lorenzo Island for the second time and foundered, on passage from the Pachacamac Islands to Huacho with 3,000 tons of guano. Her iron hull had endured 71 years at sea. The far better-known four-masted barque PAMIR had been lost in a hurricane in the North Atlantic the previous year, on 21st September 1957, while bringing grain in bulk from Buenos Aires to Europe, and only six of her complement of 86 had been saved. This tragedy suddenly terminated the efforts of the Stiftung Pamir und Passat to maintain the German tradition of cargo-carrying sail training ships, and is regarded by many as marking the end of the era of commercial deep-water sail; but it was the OMEGA which was the last great sailing ship in commercial operation, the last British-built deep-water square-rigger in service, and the last survivor of the great host of sailing ships that had thronged the nitrate and guano anchorages of the West Coast of South America.

IN THE OLD HARBOUR

'Like some medieval scene' said Dr. David Jenkins about the photographs reproduced here, which he kindly supplied from the Welsh Industrial and Maritime Museum's collection (86.153 and 86.154). They show the River Hull, the original harbour for the town of Kingston-upon-Hull, and sometimes referred to as the haven or 'Old Harbour'.

For much of Hull's early history as a port, ships had a choice of using the River Hull or discharging into lighters whilst anchored in Hull Roads. Hull's principal thoroughfare, High Street, ran along the side of the River Hull and the merchants' houses on the river side had their own private staithes where cargoes were loaded or unloaded. Inevitably, growing prosperity led to congestion in the Old Harbour, and with it demands for a dock to accommodate trading vessels. The town's first dock was completed in 1778, later to become known as Queen's Dock or the Old Dock, and which was filled in during the 1930s.

Outliving several of the docks which sought to supercede it, the tidal River Hull is still occasionally used by small ships and, as the photographs show, in the 1920s it could hold a wonderful collection of small craft. Many of these were working the inland waterways which connect with Hull, the Rivers Humber, Ouse, Trent and the Aire and Calder Navigation. The lighter lettered LNER dates the photograph opposite after the railway grouping of 1923, whilst both were taken before 1931 when the WHITE ROSE and TRENT were broken up.

These two small iron steamers were owned by the Grimsby Express Packet Co. Ltd., a company which seems to have operated regularly to a jetty on the River Hull, but is otherwise poorly recorded. Small steamers like these worked on several river systems, but only the Clyde puffers and - to a lesser extent - the Mersey and Weaver packets have been well documented. The WHITE ROSE (67/1892), seen opposite, was built at Beverley by Cochrane, Cooper and Schofield, forerunners of the well-known trawler builders. Her original owner was John Hobson of York, a reminder that this inland town was once a port. Bought by the Grimsby Express Packet Co. Ltd. in 1907, WHITE ROSE remained with them until broken up in 1931. The TRENT (107/1881), seen below, came from a small local builder, Head and Riley, of Lime Street, Hull. Her original owners were the Gainsborough United Steam Packet Co. Ltd., based right up the river after which she was named. Grimsby Express Packet Co. Ltd. acquired the TRENT in 1906 and kept her until she was demolished in 1931.

The tug BARTON (123/1891) in the photograph opposite was built by Hepple & Co. at North Shields for the Manchester, Sheffield & Lincolnshire Railway, which turned itself into the Great Central Railway in 1897, and became part of the London and North Eastern Railway at the grouping in 1923. Broken up in 1936, BARTON is recorded as spending her entire life at Grimsby, from where she has presumably arrived with lighters.

Visible in the second photograph is the steamer NUORLA (364/1918). Built at Vlaardingen near Rotterdam, she came onto the British registry in 1919, and had four owners in the space of six months before being bought by the Anglo-American Oil Co. Ltd. in 1920. She remained a dry cargo vessel throughout her 16 years with the oil company, presumably carrying motor spirit and paraffin in cans. After a spell under Danish and Latvian flags as SELMA B and OGRE, respectively, she returned to British registry in 1947, but probably saw little service and was broken up by the Rees Shipbreaking Co. Ltd. at Llanelli in 1953.

The River Hull remains an interesting backwater, but much of the activity has gone since the 1920s. Then, with its warehouses crowding the waterfront and flimsy wooden quays and mud berths, it still had echoes of the middle ages.

Thanks to Arthur Credland of Town Docks Museum, Hull for information on the River Hull.

THE COALY TYNE – SHIPPING IN THE LATE FORTIES

Captain A.W. Kinghorn

The Government's nationalisation of British coal, on 1st January 1947, brought dramatic changes not only to the miners and former coal owners but to the whole business of shipping coal by sea. For centuries coal had been carried from the north-eastern coalfields to the Thames on a private enterprise basis. Now it had to be decided - who was responsible for the large fleets of colliers (mostly ships of 1,500-2,000 tons with steam reciprocating engines powered by - what else? - coal-fired boilers), for the loading staithes and drops, the miles of railway lines taking the coal trucks along the ancient wagonways from the pits to the river, the trucks and locomotives themselves and, not least, the men who worked them?

As a measure of the number of colliers working the river at this time, during October 1946 the swing bridge at Newcastle was opened to allow 190 vessels to pass, up and down river, to the eight staithes at Derwenthaugh and Dunston. Total registered tonnage of these ships was 170,300 tons. And this was just the trade *above* Newcastle! Far more coal went out of the river from the 26 loading points lower down, at Harton, Tyne Dock, Jarrow, Pelaw, Whitehill Point, Northumberland Dock, and Howdon. I remember, one bitterly cold Saturday afternoon, standing on Harbour View - that splendid coin of vantage at the foot of Howard Street, North Shields - watching 29 deep-laden colliers putting to sea after being weather-bound by a week of south-easterly gales. As I counted them out in smoky procession I little realised that such sights would soon belong to the past as much as the collier brigs which preceded them.

Tyne trades

Import cargoes consisting of pitprops and sawn timber, grain, and a little refrigerated cargo (for instance, Tasmanian fruit in season arrived in the immaculately maintained vessels of Blue Star and Port Line). Forenede's United Shipping brought us butter from Denmark, and beer from Montrose came in Deuchar's smart little white LOCHSIDE II. There was some general cargo and petroleum products, but the iron ore berth was yet to come. Passengers were again travelling from North Shields to Bergen in the black-and-white Norwegian steamers of the Bergen Line, and to Oslo in Fred Olsen's beautiful little grey-and-white liners, each of which carried a modern metal figurehead.

Sail was represented by a few 40-year-old auxiliary schooners bringing Baltic timber, their canvas a useful means of eking out the fuel oil which was still in short supply. The Swedish three-masted steel FREJA, however, represented a class of truly modern motor schooners, cruiser-sterned, clipper-bowed and spike-bowspritted, complete with wheelhouses. It was darkly hinted that these little motor ships had only been rigged with sails to get round Swedish manning rules. Pure sail was represented by the Norwegian full-rigged training ship, SØRLANDET, which did not have an auxiliary engine when she made her first post-war visit from 14th to 17th July 1947.

Ship builders and repairers

At this time the river boasted five major shipbuilding yards: Readhead; Hawthorn Leslie; Vickers Armstrong; Swan Hunter; and Cleland. There were 45 shipbuilding berths, 27 drydocks and six slipways.

The Shipbuilding Corporation's yard at Low Walker, which had closed during the Depression, was re-opened in 1942. Empire-type cargo vessels of around 10,000 tons deadweight were built to Government account, some having flat 'coffin' transom sterns, preceding by 30 years what is now standard shipbuilding practice. Their last two hulls were sold on the stocks to United Africa, which became Palm Line, and the yard closed again in 1947. The five building yards all undertook repair work in addition to their new construction. A further six specialised in repairs and refits: these were Brigham & Cowan, Tyne Dock Engineering, Middle Docks, Mercantile, Palmers, and Smith's Docks. Engine building was the province of Parsons, Wallsend Slipway and North Eastern Marine.

All berths and drydocks were full, ships lay two and three abreast at the shipyard quays, with those which were waiting moored fore and aft to buoys. In June 1946, 194 vessels lay in the river. After six years of wartime neglect the Tyne Improvement Commission

Two views of the Norwegian training ship SØRLANDET during her visit to the Tyne 14th to 17th July 1947. In the view to the right she is passing QUEEN OF BERMUDA undergoing her post war refit. *[Author's collection]*

The little steamer LOCHSIDE II (368/1925) passes North Shields on 14th July 1954 (opposite page). She was built by Smith's Dock Co. Ltd. at Middlesbrough and served James Deuchar Ltd. of Newcastle-upon-Tyne extremely well, bringing beer from the Lochside Brewery to the Tyne for 31 years. Sold in February 1956 to Hargreaves Coal and Shipping Co. Ltd. of London, no sooner was she re-registered as HARGLEN than she was sold on to Danish owners who lost little time in fitting her with an oil engine. Thus renewed she sailed on for another two decades, as the Danish SUNDBERG and ÅNHOJ, and the Honduras-registered SIRIUS. Arrest by French authorities in May 1975 when she was off Ushant was followed by demolition at Morlaix where she arrived in May 1976. *[George Scott]*

had much to deal with as they were responsible for maintaining and improving services on the river for all its users. In addition they had to cope with the largest influx of big liners that the river had ever seen as they came in for their post-war refits. The arrival of these great ships aroused keen interest, not least amongst the schoolboy population of whom I was one. In those days the Tyne bred a large shipping community: there were few families without someone in shipbuilding, shiprepairing, or away at sea with the Royal Navy, Merchant Navy or a fishing fleet.

Malta veteran

Blue Star Line's BRISBANE STAR came in, her bow not the icebreaker or Meierform it resembled, but a hasty wartime repair of a conventional bar stem half blown off by a German torpedo on 12th August 1942. We gazed at her in awe, knowing she was one of only five survivors of the famous OHIO convoy to Malta. (Other survivors were MELBOURNE STAR, ROCHESTER CASTLE and PORT CHALMERS.) We also knew that her master, Captain F.N. Riley, had evaded the enemy by taking his ship under the cover of Cape Bon towards the Tunisian port of Sousse which was then under pro-German Vichy rule. The port authorities had sent out a boat to arrest the BRISBANE STAR for "violating neutral territory". While his men strove valiantly to repair the damage and make their vessel seaworthy, Captain Riley entertained the French naval boarding officer in his dayroom, regaling him with whisky and entente

The BRISBANE STAR arriving at Malta on 14th August 1942 (above) and the damage caused to her bow by a torpedo (below). Built by Cammell Laird & Co. Ltd. at Birkenhead in 1936, the big refrigerator ship served Blue Star Line Ltd. until 1963 when, after a voyage east as ENEA, she was broken up at Osaka. *[Imperial War Museum]*

cordiale. As the bottle was slowly emptied the BRISBANE STAR was quietly eased out of the three-mile French limit of jurisdiction, whereupon Captain Riley turned to his guest, poured him "one for the road", wished him "better fortune in happier times, m'sieur" and escorted him down to his launch. Two hundred miles further, and escorted by Spitfires, BRISBANE STAR had finally entered Valetta Grand Harbour with her cargo intact. And here she was now, on our own doorstep, bound for Palmers' Hebburn yard (part of Vickers Armstrong).

Liners come for refit

P&O's magnificent STRATHAIRD and STRATHMORE arrived at Vickers Armstrong's Naval Yard, Walker to undergo post-war conversion from grey troopships to spanking white liners. STRATHAIRD had been completed by Vickers Armstrong at Barrow in 1932 with turbo electric twin screw and three well-proportioned funnels. During the war two funnels were removed but were not replaced. We young purists felt this detracted from her appearance, but doubtless provided more space for her 1,100 passengers. STRATHMORE had been built at the same yard in 1935 with just one funnel.

When RANCHI, another P&O liner, came in between the Tyne piers for her post-war refit she was returning to her 1925 birthplace, the Hebburn yard of Hawthorn, Leslie. Sole survivor of a class of four, RANCHI's sisters were RAJPUTANA and the famous RAWALAPINDI which both sank as auxiliary cruisers, and RANPURA which was taken up by the Admiralty as a RN depot ship. RANCHI was powered by an engine arrangement which became popular with P&O in the twenties: twin-screw, quadruple-expansion with low-pressure turbines. Built with two black funnels and displaying Newcastle as the port of registry on her stern (which was unusual for P&O), her refit restored her pre-war livery of a black hull with a white line and stone-coloured superstructure, but she remained with only one funnel.

The STRATHMORE seen, not on the Tyne, but on the Mersey (above). It was not uncommon for Barrow-built ships to be sent for drydocking on the Mersey, and this Basil Feilden photograph may record the new liner's visit for this purpose.

A view of the RANCHI (left) on the Thames during her relatively brief post-war service. In January 1953 she was sold for demolition and later that month work started at the Newport yard of John Cashmore Ltd.

The DOMINION MONARCH sails from the Tyne after her post-war refit (left), and is seen dry-docked on the Tyne on a later occasion (below). Note the profusion of ships being fitted out or repaired, including the Polish BATORY. Clearly seen in the background is the covered berth where Swan Hunter & Wigham Richardson Ltd. built the MAURETANIA in 1907 *[Left: Author's collection; bottom: Tyne & Wear Archives].*

QUEEN OF BERMUDA (opposite top) and (opposite bottom) the hulk of MONARCH OF BERMUDA, 1st August 1948, being rebuilt following her disastrous fire. *[Both: World Ship Photo Library]*

Shaw Savill's two-funnelled DOMINION MONARCH returned to her 1939 builders, Swan Hunter at Wallsend. Although I missed seeing her come in, I saw her ready to sail, all gleaming paint and varnish, decks scrubbed, polished brass winking in the sun. She returned to the service for which she had been built, outward from London to New Zealand via South Africa with 500 passengers and general cargo, homeward across the Pacific through the Panama Canal with passengers and refrigerated cargo. A magnificent ship, known to seafarers as the DM, her quadruple screws driven by internal combustion engines made her one of the world's largest motorships.

Furness Withy's handsome twin sisters, MONARCH OF BERMUDA and QUEEN OF BERMUDA, which had been built at Walker by Vickers in 1931 and 1933, arrived to grace the scene. The famous hammerhcad crane which was installed to build the MONARCH stands to this day, having been used ever since to build and refit ships. Before the war quadruple-screw, turbo-electric machinery drove these ships at 20 knots and carried their 730 passengers in sumptuous style between New York and Hamilton, Bermuda. Now, after wartime trooping service, they were to be restored to pre-war magnificence. The QUEEN's forward funnel was lengthened by four feet and her after funnel shortened by the same amount, which improved her rather flat-topped thirties look when all three funnels were the same height.

Fire and its aftermath

The same treatment would perhaps have been accorded to the MONARCH but late in the afternoon of 24th March 1947 fire broke out on board while she was lying in the Palmers' Hebburn drydock.

The firefloat SALVOR (left) and the paddle tug COBLE DENE (below) were involved in efforts to fight the fire on the MONARCH OF BERMUDA. Built of iron by Hepple in 1883, the 125gt COBLE DENE was owned by the Tyne Improvement Commissioners. The paddle tug is seen in July 1953 in Northumberland Dock, with what appears to be a sailing ship in the distance. COBLE DENE was broken up in the mid 1950s. Note the figure 8 on the funnel. *[George Scott]*

Shipyard fire-fighting was immediately employed but the blaze was not extinguished until the following afternoon. Men and equipment from the National Fire Service worked mainly from the paddle tug COBLE DENE and the firefloats PATROL and SALVOR. Restoration to her pre-war condition was now out of the question and she was taken over by the Australian government, refitted to carry immigrants, and placed under the management of Shaw Savill, Furness's associated company. Under her new and aptly chosen name, NEW AUSTRALIA, she carried thousands of families out to their new home under the assisted passage scheme. She was also used as a troopship in the Korean War. In 1951 the QUEEN OF BERMUDA was joined by a new, single-funnelled sister, the OCEAN MONARCH, running a joint service until replaced in the mid sixties by the ubiquitous jet airliner.

The GEORGIC, the last of the big post-war refits, arrived at Palmers' Hebburn yard in July 1948. Dating from 1932, she was the last ship built for White Star Line before its Government-enforced merger with Cunard in 1934 (to obtain the much-needed subsidy for the new liner QUEEN MARY building at John Brown). GEORGIC had spent most of the war as a troopship. On 14th July 1941 she went on fire at Port Tewfik, the southern entrance to the Suez Canal. I sailed as a cadet with a second mate who had been an AB when the GEORGIC had that fire. He and another sailor had been trapped near the foremast. There was a carley float life-raft lashed in the rigging but my second mate had nothing with which to cut it free. Fortunately the other sailor had a knife and they were able to escape the inferno. On the strength of that story I have carried a knife ever since.

After the fire GEORGIC had been towed to Port Sudan for temporary repairs. At Karachi she underwent further repairs, sufficient to get her home to her builders, Harland & Wolff. Permanent conversion into a troopship followed, in which she

GEORGIC at Liverpool soon after the war.

forfeited one of her two funnels and one mast, and thereafter ran until the end of hostilities for the Ministry of War Transport. During her Tyne refit she was converted to carry 2,000 immigrant passengers and, like NEW AUSTRALIA, was placed on the UK-Australia/New Zealand service, with occasional trooping. Her last trip was to bring British troops home from Japan in 1956, after which she was broken up at Faslane.

Real sailormen

On 29th October 1946 another graceful old ship arrived at Swan Hunter's for refit. Much smaller and very different from the lordly liners, she arrived in tow from the Humber, where she had lain idle since bringing in a load of Australian grain in 1939. One of Gustav Erikson's famous fleet of square riggers, this four-masted barque, ARCHIBALD RUSSELL, was to be refitted and rerigged, then put back into service. Immediately after the war tonnage was in desperately short supply and cargo for sailing ships was still available in some trades.

I and a few like-minded pals decided we would sail in her - as *real* sailormen! (We knew that in their later years Erikson's ships were often crewed by teenagers.) Our local newspaper reported that a survey had found her in remarkably good condition. Captain Erikson visited his old ship and put the work in hand, but it would be a long job. Materials were in short supply, as too were the men skilled in refitting sailing ships. The longer the work took however, the older, and consequently perhaps more eligible, we would be. But when Captain Erikson died suddenly in August 1947 our plans fell through, to our mortification. Laid up to buoys at Dunston she was broken up by J.J. King on the Gateshead foreshore in 1949.

Our wanderings up to see the ARCHIBALD RUSSELL took us to this foreshore, where we found the tide-waterlogged hulk of an old wooden brig, blackened with age and rot. Her name, we learned, was VINDEX and it was clear she had lain there many years. The hull was more or less intact, her two masts cut off at deck level, but the ship's side chain plates showed what her rig had been. (Equal numbers of dead-eyes at fore and main clearly indicated that both masts were once square-rigged.) We climbed down into the after cabin and could picture a master and his mate making themselves at home there. In the triangular hovel forward the six bunks in pairs left little space for even the crew's mess table. Doubtless when we returned home our mothers wondered what the smell was!

One ship which missed her post-war refit was the Greek steamer ZEPHYROS, which dragged from her anchorage off the river in a snowstorm on the night of 25th/26th February 1947. The following afternoon we were given time off school to go and see her, hard and fast off Brown's Point, Cullercoats, little more than a biscuit's toss from Cullercoats radio station. Under the Greek flag and with Piraeus painted across her counter stern, she still carried the Ritson's of Sunderland blue-and-white striped funnel from her CHERRY BRANCH days. All else was drab wartime grey. On that heavily overcast, stormy afternoon a tug and the Tynemouth and Cullercoats lifeboats were standing by. Tynemouth Volunteer Life Brigade got lines aboard and rigged their breeches buoy, all communications with the shore being made by flashing morse lamp. But when the tide receded her crew walked ashore across the flat rocks to safety.

Eventually, of course, we went aboard her, scrambling into the engine room through a rectangular hole of some cooling water inlet. An unforgettable sight, she lay port side towards the coast, head in, masking the large hole torn in her starboard side as she came over the rocks. This hole illuminated the engine room in a weird greenish light in which the tall reciprocating engine stood draped with seaweed, the bottom plates littered with sand and stones over which crabs scuttled. Gingerly climbing the narrow steel ladders, we visited the tiny wheelhouse and then made our way forward. A huge Admiralty Pattern anchor was stowed on the port side of the forecastle head with its crane 'ready for use', just as we had seen on the ARCHIBALD RUSSELL. Her two stockless anchors were missing, presumably lost in the storm.

Attempts to refloat her failed. She had gone ashore on the top of a very high tide, a light ship which could not be lightened because she had no ballast on board and very little in her bunkers. Eventually broken up where she lay, she had cost the life of at least one sightseer, who ventured aboard one night and fell into a flooded hold.

Compared with those days, the Coaly Tyne now seems a very quiet river!

The Greek steamer ZEPHYROS aground off Cullercoats in February 1947 (top). Built in 1909 by Charles Connell & Co. at Glasgow as DUNEDIN, she had been a handy-sized steamer of 4,796 tons in her day, sold to Ritson's Branch Line in 1919 to become CHERRY BRANCH (below) and going to Greece in 1931. *[Top: Author's collection; bottom: World Ship Photo Library]*

Cullercoats, North Shields, Tyne & Wear NE30 3AQ

John Naylon has found two records of MOZART calling at Queenstown for orders during the period FAILTE was in service. On 19th July 1927, the year FAILTE was bought, MOZART arrived after a 152-day voyage from Port Lincoln, proceeding to Hull for discharge. Her second arrival, on 5th June 1929, followed a much better passage, 119 days from Wallaroo. MOZART then discharged at Le Havre.

French correction

May I offer some additional information on a ship featured in *Record 7*? The German DUISBURG was handed over to the Société Générale de Transports Maritimes à Vapeur but was found to be in poor condition and laid up at Marseilles. In fact, she did not trade under their flag, and was broken up at Toulon in January 1924. It was not at all unusual for ex-German ships to keep their original names until they were actually transferred to the management or ownership of a company.

R.R.Y.N. MALO, 22 Stonehenge Road, Amesbury, Wiltshire SP4 7BA.

A two flag problem

Having enjoyed *Record 7,* I would like to add a comment to the 'two flag' debate. The flag flown by German vessels, as observed on the Thames in 1947, was, in fact, a fixed metal plate 'flown' from the ensign staff and was the international code flag 'C' (horizontal bands of blue, white, red, white, and blue). This was understood to indicate that the vessels were in the hands of the Allied Control Commission, whose title gave rise to many of the 'Empire' names allocated to ex-Axis vessels such as EMPIRE **CON**FAL, **CON**EXE, **CON**CAVE. I never recall seeing any other national flag so displayed, and certainly vessels such as GERHARD (Mathies Reederei), KOLBERG (R.C. Gribel), and HOHEWEG (W. Schuchmann) did not, but did display a Commission number below the name on the bow.

ALAN E. PHIPPS, 2 Riverside Road, Droitwich Spa, Worcester WR9 8UW.

I am probably not the first to notice that BEGONIA (*Record 6)* is in a river and not flying a courtesy flag. It could be that for some reason she is flying the courtesy ensign inferior to her national flag. If you know the location of the photograph then you may be half way there – but it could be French or Belgian waters. I have never seen this done with national and courtesy ensigns, but I have certainly done it with houseflags. Ben Lines' BENVORLICH was often on long-term charter to Lauritzen Bulkers back in the late 1970s and 1980s, and we always flew the owner's flag on the same halliard but superior to the Lauritzen flag.

BARRY STANDERLINE, 5 Woodville House, Woodville, By Arbroath, Angus DD11 3RH

This is any interesting suggestion, but the photograph of BEGONIA was taken in the Mersey, not in French or Belgian waters.

A one flag problem

May I include among the many deserved congratulations to your periodical, my own for your policy of giving due mention to the funnel markings and houseflags worn by the vessels in your excellent photographs. In the article on the Wanstead-class ships in *Record 6,* you attribute the funnel of WENDOVER in the top photograph to a Port Line charter. This may well be so, and the grey hull lends credence to it, but whatever the houseflag at the maintruck may be, it is certainly not the cross and saltire of the Port Line, dating back to the days of the old Tyser Line. I first thought the lighter device on the dark flag might be the Cunard lion and globe, which would tally with the funnel; but the device seems too close to the hoist of the flag for this. Perhaps an enlargement, or another reader's contribution, might solve this little problem?

J.L. LOUGHRAN, 333 Streetsbrook Road, Solihull, West Midlands B91 1RW

Gas turbines: a false dawn

With regard to John Lamb's experimental gas turbine installation in the tanker AURIS and what is recalled as a free-piston gasifier/turbine combination in the ore carrier MORAR (see *Record 6* and *7*), they cannot be said to have set much of a trend for British merchant ships. Only now are gas turbines finding some favour in fast ferry applications, the speed gained offset by fuel consumption requiring good loading to justify it. On the other hand, Jackie Fisher's plea to engineers of his day to devise an internal combustion turbine for warships has been well answered for half a century, the first Royal Navy application being the Metropolitan-Vickers installation in a motor gunboat in 1947. Today's warships thus enjoy low stand-by costs, fast start-up, and machinery layouts giving cruising and high-speed performances applicable to their duties.

With the benefit of hindsight, John Lamb's greatest work was surely his parallel experiments leading to the successful burning of 'residual' fuel oils in the reciprocating diesel engines of the 12,000 deadweight, 4,400 IHP tanker AURICULA in 1947; such fuels being the residue of the distillation process in which lighter

Seen on her native Clyde, the MORAR was built in 1959 by Lithgows Ltd., Port Glasgow for Scottish Ore Carriers Ltd., a company in which Lithgows were the largest shareholders, although as managers Denholms also had a financial interest. Her gas-turbine machinery was clearly experimental, and after just two years it was replaced with another gas-turbine. But even this did not last that long and, on her sale to German owners in 1967, the ore carrier was fitted with a diesel engine. Renamed first CLARI, and after 1969 ARNIS, she remained under German control until sale to Indonesia as MAHONI in 1974. Her relatively modern engines should have given her a long life, but on 26th September 1979 the MAHONI ran aground in the strait between the Philippines and Taiwan. With her engine room flooded and her cement cargo solidifying, she became a constructive total loss.

fractions are extracted from the crude. Diesel engines working on the air-blast method of injecting fuel to the cylinders could be made to burn virtually any kind of liquid fuel, this being a desirable attribute in early days since oil-fuel bunkering stations offering standard grades did not exist worldwide. Around 1930, however, in search of higher thermal and mechanical efficiency, designers turned back to the older 'solid injection' method, depending on a pump and spray nozzle; but for reliability these demanded clean distilled fuel which was more expensive, if by then more widely available. Lamb's triumph lay in devising a means by which this system could burn the cheaper fuel, and in that he owed much to the centrifugal oil separator devised by Gustav de Laval. The system is now widely applied, its coming sounding the death knell of steamships in merchant service.

IAN W. MUIR, 2 Chapelton Cottage, Udny, Ellon, Aberdeenshire AB41 6PX.

Issues in *Record*

Although I agree with the article in *Record 5* which mentions the very high standard of accommodation on the Wanstead class ships of Watts Watts, the location of many of the cabins on the inboard side meant that off-duty crew could not get much sleep when cargo was being worked. The side opening hatches as illustrated in the booklet meant that the deck was very congested when working cargo and that deck cargo space was at a premium. This would have been a major drawback when carrying general cargo – including hazardous cargo requiring open deck stowage – for a range of ports. WIMBLEDON had the same type of hatch lids.

In regard to Paul Boot's letter on split superstructures (see *Record 6*), the bridge of the MICHIGAN is actually amidships because the load lines are visible below the bridge wing. Whilst I agree that the design was commonly referred to as three-quarters aft, I would point out that the design was comparatively rare. I think that MICHIGAN would have been a very difficult ship to load with general break bulk cargo. It is interesting that these four vessels, built to CGT order, were the first to have split superstructures for nearly 30 years and that the layout was not used in subsequent vessels. I subscribe to Paul's comments about blind adherence to old-established practices both in design, and – indeed – in procedures in shipping companies up to the mid-1960s.

In *Record 7,* David Burrell's comment understates the status of the Guinness ships registered in what was then Eire. The facts are that the British Government refused to recognise the Irish Tricolour and there were a number of prosecutions of masters of ships flying this flag. It was not until the Second World War that the 'Free State' or 'Eire' flag became accepted. At this time the LM&S railway re-registered its vessels in London. Prior to this they had been registered in Dublin but had continued to fly the Red Ensign and were described as British in *Lloyd's Register.*

GEOFFREY HOLMES, 17 Bayswater Court, Newport Avenue, Wallasey, Wirral, Cheshire L45 8QJ.

CAM not MAC

DUNKERY BEACON on page 140 of *Record 7* was one of the two Y-type Empire ships built by Cammell Laird, the other being the EMPIRE CLIVE, which I knew well as the CHARLBURY of Alexander Shipping Company. It was always rather puzzled that this pair, built about 18 months into the Second World War, were not more austere. The ships had well-raked stems, full cruiser sterns, and curved bridge fronts. The rounded bridge structure is well illustrated in the photograph and is identical to that of the CHARLBURY. This leads me to query the statement that EMPIRE FLAME had been converted into a merchant aircraft carrier. It was the Cammell Laird-built EMPIRE MACCOLL which served as an aircraft carrier and later became BRITISH PILOT.

I wonder about the purpose of the two tubular 'struts' which appear to be propping up the foremast of DUNKERY BEACON? There is no jumbo derrick fitted to the mast, which might have justified the fitting of apparently extra supports.

The photograph of BEACONSFIELD reminded me of two distinctive features of Watts, Watts' pre-war ships. They all sported large cross-trees on the fore topmasts, which were twice as big as was normal for other tramps of that period. And, although not visible in your photo, these ships had small weather vanes on each top-mast. Sailing ship practice, I guess, but why?

I wonder how many people recall that, besides having transom sterns, the Elder Dempster 'New' class of cargo ship in 1919 were fitted with square-section derrick posts. These are hardly discernible in the photograph of NEW BROOKLYN (page 189) and I cannot recall any other British ships so fitted. During the Second World War some U.S.-built C2 cargo ships had square-section masts and derricks, as did a number of post-war Dutch cargo liners.

I offer an observation about a structural change which the LADY SYLVIA underwent upon changing ownership. The two pictures of her on pages 151 and 155 show that, in order to facilitate cargo working by shore cranes, the derricks and winches have been dispensed with, and the mast re-positioned at the break of the forecastle. In addition, a new raised cargo hatch has been fitted between number 1 and number 2 hatches. Presumably, the new hatch would be above the bulkhead between number 1 and number 2 holds, but it would give better access for loading coal between the ends of these two hatch coamings and the hold bulkhead, a space which it is normally only possible to fill completely by employing trimmers, or by using angled coal chutes.

JOHN B. HILL, The Hollies, Wall, Hexham, Northumberland NE46 4EQ.

Derek Atherton of St. Helens also wrote to point out that EMPIRE FLAME was a catapult-armed merchantman (CAM) and not a MAC, and that only tankers and grain ships were converted to merchant aircraft carriers

Not under the influence

Seven readers have written to tell us that the structure on the bridge of JESSIE on page 170 of Record 7 *is designed to lift the standard compass as high as possible, so it was not under the magnetic influence of the iron hull, funnel and ventilators. Ivor Rooke recalls a description in* Sea Breezes, *November 1952, page 315, of how the newly-appointed master of the ship RIBSTON, which had frequently been going aground, noticed that there was a significant movement of the compass when one of the ventilators was moved to face the wind.*

A pole-mounted compass in front of the bridge was carried by some deep-sea trawlers in the 1930s. Brunel went further, with a compass mounted on top of one of the GREAT EASTERN's masts, which raises the question of how was it read. With a pole compass, after each course alteration and at the end of each watch, a seaman would climb the ladder to check the steering compass against the standard compass, although sometimes a periscope was fitted. Thanks to David Edge, John B. Hill, Dr. David Jenkins, Paul M. König, Sutherland Manson, Ivor Rooke, and Tony Smythe.

Enlightenment

*The query about the structures on the forecastle of HUBBUCK (*Record 7, *pages 168-9) has brought forth more letters than any other topic we have mentioned in* Record. *Rather than single out one or two letters for* *publication, we summarise here the information received from a number of readers who were unanimous in their opinions.*

The structures which look like white lighthouses are, in fact, white lighthouses. They protected the port and starboard navigation lights – the sidelights – and evolved with the sailing ship. These lighthouses were so positioned that the red and green lights could be seen through the prescribed sector angle – normally from dead ahead to two points astern of abeam – and were not obscured by the fore course when this sail was set.

These lighthouses were quite commonly fitted not only to sailing ships but also to steamers which carried sail in the latter part of the nineteenth century, and HUBBUCK was certainly fully-rigged when built in 1886. They can also be discerned on OVINGDEAN GRANGE and HORNBY GRANGE on page 134, BUTESHIRE page 135, READY page 160, and MOUNT LEBANON page 167 of the same issue. It was only when sails were eliminated from steamships that their sidelights could be positioned aft of the foremast, and could thus be incorporated into the wings of the bridge or other superstructure. Prior to this, it was the lookout's job to report 'lights abright, sir.'

The lighthouses could be quite elaborate affairs, with burnished copper domes, although if neglected these could easily become a dull green colour. A drawing sent by Tony Smythe shows the port lighthouse as fitted to the paddle steamer LA MARGUERITE. This shows the protruding rectangular screen, which is well seen in the starboard view of the HUBBUCK.

To service the lights, the lamptrimmer gained entry via a hole in the lamproom in the forecastle, and thus avoided the hazards of venturing onto the forecastle in a seaway. In some cases, the lighthouses or 'pepperpots' also contained the heads. Admitting a man was one factor in their size, another being the rise of the forecastle ahead of them: those in HUBBUCK seeming particularly large.

For enlightening the editors on this subject we thank Captain N.E. Banner, Michael Charles, Alex Duncan, David Edge, John B. Hill, John Holliday, John B. Hood, Fred Kilgour, Captain A.W. Kinghorn, Paul M. König, Sutherland Mason, C.J. Moore, James Pottinger, Ivor Rooke, Tony Smythe and Urbain Ureel.

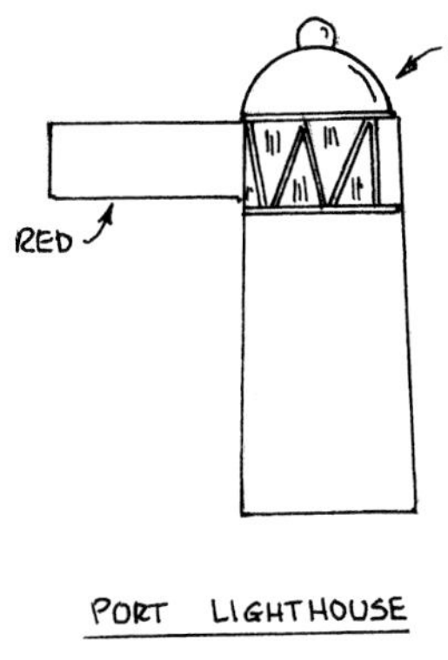

Tony Smythe's drawing of the lighthouse on the LA MARGUERITE (2,205/1894). The paddle steamer, shown above on the Mersey in later life, had an interesting career, and Frank Thornley's *Steamers of North Wales* records that she was built to offer day excursions between Tilbury, Margate and Boulogne. She was named after the daughter of one of her owners, presumably made to sound French because of her intended service.

As the photograph shows, LA MARGUERITE was huge, and at 342 feet overall was bigger than many contemporary ocean-going cargo ships. She was licensed to carry three thousand passengers to Margate, and two thousand onwards across the Channel. LA MARGUERITE is claimed to have been the largest pleasure steamer to sail on the Thames and the second largest paddler to operate on British coastal services. Indeed, there are stories that, whilst operating excursions to North Wales from the landing stage at Liverpool, she was boarded on several occasions by passengers who thought she was about to cross the Atlantic.

The original owners of LA MARGUERITE are given as Palace Steamers Ltd., and managers the Victoria Steamboat Association Ltd., but Palace very soon failed, and ownership quickly reverted to the paddler's builders. Although New Palace Steamers Ltd. was soon incorporated to take over the failed company's services, the paddler remained under the ownership of Fairfield Shipbuilding and Engineering Co. Ltd. This may have played a part in her 1904 transfer to Liverpool for excursions to North Wales, owners becoming the Liverpool and North Wales Steamship Co. Ltd. in whom Fairfields had an interest.

On the North Wales service LA MARGUERITE became well loved, especially towards the end of her career. Her last excursion from Liverpool to Llandudno and Menai Bridge was made on 28th September 1925. In her final years she suffered various minor breakdowns, and Thornley believed that hard wartime service as a cross-Channel troopship had taken its toll. The steamer was sold to T.W. Ward Ltd. and sailed from Liverpool for the very last time on 22nd September 1925, bound for the breakers' yard at Briton Ferry. A small deck house was removed from LA MARGUERITE for use on the pier at Llandudno: it would be interesting to know how long this survived.

RECORD BOOKS

Record does not review books: we have reservations about one publisher reviewing the output of another, and feel that the monthly magazines do the job in a more timely fashion than we can. However, in line with our historical bent we would like to look back occasionally at books that are held in particular affection. They might be books that changed the way we looked at ships, or the way we thought about maritime history, or that have stood the test of time and have become classics. Contributions for this occasional column are welcome.

Old Order, New Thing by H. Campbell McMurray, H.M.S.O.

When I noticed *Old Order, New Thing* on sale for just 50p in the National Maritime Museum's bookshop, I wondered how anyone could possibly write enough about one paddle tug to fill sixty pages and three appendices. Having read it, I wondered how H. Campbell McMurray had managed to get everything he had say into so few pages. And I learned an important lesson about industrial history.

The paddle tug RELIANT, born as the Manchester Ship Canal's OLD TRAFFORD and then (1972) recently installed in the New Neptune Hall at Greenwich, is the star of the book, in that everything revolves round her. How tug building became an important industry on the Tyne, and how her builder Joseph T. Eltringham's yard was founded, are just two of the preliminaries to discussing the design of the OLD TRAFFORD. One of the charms, and indeed marvels, of the book is that technicalities are handled in such a way as to be comprehensible to anyone who takes a little trouble to follow the discussion. This demands a determination on the part of the author both to fully master the principles concerned, and to put in the effort to explain them in a way which enlightens the non-specialist reader without horrifying a passing engineer. And technological developments are not presented in the gee whiz, *Tomorrow's World* fashion which implies that anyone who doesn't adopt them will soon be an object of derision, or bankrupt, or both. Read, for instance, McMurray on the feathering paddle wheel or the side-lever steam engine, their benefits and drawbacks, and you have an insight into why the latest innovation is not always the best solution to a given problem. For the OLD TRAFFORD with her paddles, archaic engine, and low boiler pressure was by no means the last word in marine technology in 1907. Yet for her purpose as stern tug in guiding ships down the canal to Manchester, the author suggests she and her fellow paddle tugs have never been surpassed.

The author never lets the star steal the show. Indeed, for the first few scenes OLD TRAFFORD does not feature at all. The book begins with a succinct account of why and how the Manchester Ship Canal came to be be built, familiar ground maybe, but handled with the rigour of a modern economic historian. The author returns to review the larger picture towards the end, and asks if the canal was really worth building. His answer is a qualified yes. The canal was hardly ever used for its avowed purpose of importing cotton, but its existence did stimulate the growth of other industries alongside the waterway – including engineering, oil refining, chemicals – which have sustained the region's economy when its traditional textile industry declined.

Perhaps the most fascinating chapter concerns the crewing of Ship Canal tugs. A picture is drawn of men who were never more than 20 miles from their homes (these were almost invariably in Runcorn, which the tugs passed daily) but who might be away from them for weeks at a stretch. The sociology of the tug crew is explored, and especially how a 'lad' would be introduced to the job, and – thanks to the oddly closed community – in all probability stay on the same tug throughout his working life. There is considerably less on the employment of the tug from 1950, when she left the canal and went to work in the north east as the RELIANT, but this probably reflects the effort put into researching the employment for which OLD TRAFFORD was designed.

Modern industrial historians tend to stress the importance of context. Although Campbell McMurray hardly if ever employs the word, his book is an object lesson in putting an artefact – in this case a preserved tug – into its engineering, maritime, economic and social contexts. In his epilogue, he stresses that '. . . the industrial archaeologist should never be satisfied simply and solely with his assorted bits and pieces . . . He must go further than that, to considering in what ways his work can be brought to bear on the myriad of unresolved questions littering the path of industrial change. And this he can accomplish only by locating his studies, from the beginning, firmly within the broad framework of economic and industrial activity.' If we enthusiasts for maritime history want to get the most out of our interest we should not be content with viewing a ship as merely a ship, no matter how attractive she looks. We ought to look at her as well as an expression of the naval architect's and marine engineer's art, as an investment by her owner who intended to get a return from her, as the home for the men who sailed her, and as a unit which carried a tiny part of the world's trade.

Campbell McMurray got one thing rather badly wrong. He refers to the New Neptune Hall at the National Maritime Museum as 'her last resting place', but this was not to be. In a classic case of having more money than sense, the National Maritime Museum has spent £11 million of National Lottery money on replacing this Hall, and only the engine of the old RELIANT has a place in the new order of things. At present the hull of the only paddle tug we British have ever managed to preserve lies in a South London yard, in the hope that another museum may take it on.

Whilst there are those who will chide the National Maritime Museum for not keeping its promises on preserving the RELIANT, there are lessons to be learnt. The first is that tucking an artefact as large as a tug away in a museum does not ensure its preservation for posterity, however much we would wish otherwise. The second lesson is that the knowledge and insights packed into Campbell McMurray's book really are there for posterity, or at least for as long as libraries last. A senior maritime historian has said that if as much effort was put into safeguarding documentary sources as goes into preserving ships, we would know a lot more about maritime history. The history of the RELIANT has proved him right. *RSF*

RELIANT in service for the Ridley Steam Tug Co. Ltd. after her sale by the Manchester Ship Canal in September 1950 (top). In his splendid *150 Years of the Maltese Cross,* John Proud records that Ridleys bought her for £1,650 and sold her six years later for £4,000. New owners in September 1956 were the Seaham Harbour Dock Company and in the photograph on the left she is slipped in their colours. She was sold to the National Maritime Museum in June 1969, and towed to Cory's barge yard at Charlton on the Thames to be made ready for display.

The paddle tug was altered after arriving on the Tyne, most noticeably by being given a larger funnel, which is why she remained as RELIANT in the National Maritime Museum rather than reverting to her original name of OLD TRAFFORD.

SOURCES AND ACKNOWLEDGEMENTS

Photographs are from the collection of John Clarkson unless otherwise credited. We thank all who gave permission for their photographs to be used, and are particularly grateful to David Whiteside and Tony Smith of the World Ship Photo Library; and to Ivor Rooke, George Scott, Peter Newall, and the museums and institutions listed for help in finding photographs.

In researching captions, sources have included the *Registers* of William Schell and Tony Starke, *Lloyd's Register, Lloyd's Confidential Index, Lloyd's War Losses, Mercantile Navy Lists* and *Marine News.* Use of the facilities of the World Ship Society's Central Record, the Guildhall Library and Lloyd's Register of Shipping are gratefully acknowledged. Particular thanks also to William Schell and John Bartlett for information and to Heather Fenton for editorial services.

Two funnel cargo liners

Books consulted include *Deutsche-Australische Dampschiffs-Gesellschaft* by Reinhart Schmelzkopf (Strandgut, 1984, Cuxhaven), *Merchant Ships of the World in Colour 1910-1929* by Laurence Dunn (Blandford, 1973, London), and *Frank C. Strick & Co.* JEB Belt & HS Appleyard (WSS, 1996, Kendal).

British yard, Greek tramp

Malcolm Cranfield, Louis Loughran and Lawrence Dunn kindly commented on earlier drafts of this article. Two books proved useful: *A History of Greek-owned Shipping* by Gelina Harlaftis (Routledge, London, 1996) and *Ships Loved and Painted* by Manuel Kulukundis (Krikos, London, 1977).

Tower Shipping

Thanks are due particularly to Mr Ted Deadman and the staff of Lloyd's Register of Shipping and the Guildhall Library.

OMEGA – the last of her race

A brief history of the Drum Line is provided by Basil Lubbock in *The Last of the Windjammers,* Vol. II (Brown, Son & Ferguson, Glasgow, 1960). The fortunes of the German sail fleet can be followed in 'Die alte deutsche Segelschiffs-Flotte', *Der Albatros,* Heft 4 (1957/III), pp.21-3 and in *To Santa Rosalia, Further and Back* by Harold D. Huycke Jr. (The Mariners Museum, Newport News, Virginia, 1990). The career of the OMEGA is described in *Hamburgs Segelschiffe 1795-1945* by Jürgen Meyer (Egon Heinemann, Norderstedt, 1980, pp.172, 174), in F.D. Wilhelmsen, *Omega: Last of the Barques* (The Newman Press, USA, 1956) and in William Kooiman, 'Omega – last of the guano traders', *Der Albatros,* Heft 2, 1993, 38 Jahrgang, pp.40-6.

The tanker that never was

Dr Ian Buxton's kind assistance in providing data from berth lists at the Walker Naval Yard is gratefully acknowledged.

Post-war South African Coasters

Many thanks to Jimmy Smith who kindly lent comprehensive fleet lists of South African coasters and to Brian Ingpen, author of *South African Merchant Ships.*

POST-WAR SOUTH AFRICAN COASTERS

Peter Newall

Up to the early 1950s, coastal shipping in South Africa was a very haphazard affair, with few shipping companies and many old ships. Apart from the treacherous weather conditions which the tiny ships frequently experienced along the coast, the coaster operators had to contend with the so-called sea competitive railway rates which the South African Government imposed to coax shippers to move their cargoes by rail, rather than the shorter sea routes between major coastal centres. All this changed in 1954, however, with the abolition of the scheme and the various lines rapidly built up their fleets with many interesting secondhand ships – the focus of this pictorial feature. By the 1960s, the three major lines started replacing their fleets with more up-to-date tonnage and, in 1966, they merged their resources to form Unicorn Shipping Lines and this was the start of the modern coasting era for South Africa.

THE COASTAL WHITE STAR

The oldest of all the South African coastal companies was the Thesen Steamship Company, founded by the Norwegian Thesen family who in 1870 settled in Knysna, a small port between Cape Town and Port Elizabeth. Knysna owed its existence to large local indigenous forests, and Thesens soon dominated this timber trade. In 1921, the family sold the shipping business to the Houston Line of Liverpool who, like all subsequent purchasers up to 1966, kept the Thesen name and colours, black funnel with red band and white star. Sold in 1936 to Mitchell Cotts & Co. Ltd., Thesens was taken over in 1952 by a specially-formed subsidiary of Coast Lines, Coast Lines Africa (Pty.) Ltd., and all the ships were given -COAST names. In 1966 Safmarine bought the company and subsequently sold the entire fleet to the newly-formed Unicorn Lines in exchange for a 27% shareholding in Unicorn.

AGNAR
Stavanger Stöberi & Dok, Stavanger, Norway; 1884, 427gt, 151 feet
This tiny ship was the first steamer owned by the Thesen family and was purchased secondhand in 1896. Sometimes known as the 'Knysna Mail Packet', AGNAR also had accommodation for 18 first class passengers amidships, although the term first class was a bit of a misnomer as the ship had limited catering facilities on board. Sold in 1936 to the Eagle Shipping Co., Mauritius, two years later, with a cargo of coal and cattle on a voyage from Madagascar to Mauritius, she was lost in a cyclone with all hands. *[Martin Leendertz Collection, S.A. Library]*

ZULU COAST
Ardrossan Dockyard Ltd., Ardrossan; 1957, 813gt, 161 feet
Despite modern navigation equipment, the motorship ZULU COAST was also lost at sea although all her crew were saved. Ironically, this ship was built to cope with the difficult operating conditions on the treacherous west coast, where many ships were wrecked because of gales and shifting sandbars. The cold Benguela Current also produces thick banks of fog and it was in one of these in 1971 that the ZULU COAST, now known as ZULU, collided with her running mate OVAMBO and sank. *[Peter Newall Collection]*

BASUTO COAST (top)
De Haan & Oerlemans Scheepsbouwerf, Heusden, Netherlands; 1937, 246gt, 99 feet
This motorship was originally DURNESS, one of an identical pair ordered from the Dutch yard by Ovenstone Coasters for their fishing business on the west coast. Bought by Thesens in 1941 with her sister DALNESS (later NAMAQUA COAST), she was chartered to the Ministry of War Transport for use as a cargo carrier in the Red Sea and the Mediterranean. Returned to her owner in 1948, she was renamed BASUTO and then BASUTO COAST in 1953. A year later, after an engine failure, she suffered the indignity of being wrecked opposite the popular Sea Point swimming pool in Cape Town in one of the Cape's infamous winter north gales, not far from the spot where the SA SEAFARER was lost 12 years later in a similar storm – see *Record 4* – page 205. *[Peter Newall Collection]*

MASHONA COAST (middle)
Furness Shipbuilding Co. Ltd., Haverton Hill-on-Tees; 1944, 413gt, 142 feet
In 1945, the Union Steamship Co. of South Africa was formed by a group of ex-servicemen and rapidly built up a small fleet of ships before their take-over by the Thesens company in 1949. One of these ships was OKIEP, bought in 1947, and which had been the Ministry of War Transport coastal tanker CHANT 44. She was one of over 40 prefabricated CHANT tankers constructed in 1944 for use during the Allied invasion of Europe, and which were designed for easy beaching. CHANT 44 was sold in 1946 to Greek owners who converted her into the dry cargo ship ANDRONIKI. Renamed MASHONA in 1946, after the formation of Coast Lines Africa, she became MASHONA COAST in 1953. Operating mainly on the Cape Town-Walvis Bay run, she was sold in 1964 to the Marine Diamond Corporation who used her for a year as a barge before she was scrapped. *[Peter Newall Collection]*

GRIQUA COAST (bottom)
S.P. Austin & Sons Ltd., Sunderland; 1935, 594 gt, 196 feet
An archetypal engines-aft Coast Lines motorship of the 1930s, GRIQUA COAST was built as ANGLIAN COAST in 1935. In March 1941, she hit a mine near the Bar Light Vessel, Liverpool and was later repaired. Her UK service ended in 1955 when she was chartered to Coast Lines Africa as GRIQUA COAST and became the flagship of the fleet. In 1958 she started a cargo service between Durban and Walvis Bay, and was transferred to the Cape Town register in 1961. Withdrawn from service in 1966, she was towed from Cape Town to nearby Saldanha Bay by PONDO COAST for demolition. *[Peter Newall Collection]*

AFRICAN COASTERS

From humble beginnings in 1933, African Coasters (Pty.) Ltd. of Durban developed in the 1950s and 1960s into South Africa's largest coaster company. After the abolition of the restrictive sea competitive rates scheme in 1954, the company bought a number of interesting ships to service their expanding route network.

CECILE MAPLESON (top)
Bow, McLachlan & Co. Ltd., Paisley; 1924, 344gt, 143 feet
This veteran started life as the twin-screw motorship HALAL, a London-registered pilgrim ship owned by the Cowasjee family and based in the Red Sea. In 1933 she became the first ship owned by the newly-formed African Coasters (Pty.) Ltd. Given the stage name of the professional singer wife of one of the founding directors, CECILE MAPLESON was used mainly on the Durban-East London-Port Elizabeth trade. In 1941 she was requisitioned by the Admiralty and converted into a harbour defence cableship, and given stump masts with derricks port and starboard for lifting ASDIC units. Returned to her owners in 1946, she was sold in 1952 to South African interests and in 1955, 22 years after the start of African Coasters, she became the first in the fleet of Durban Coasters (later known as Durban Lines) which had been formed to operate a feeder service between Durban and Moçambique ports. Renamed CONGELLA, she was broken up in Durban in 1964. *[Peter Newall Collection]*

RANGE (middle)
Caledon Shipbuilding & Engineering Co. Ltd., Dundee; 1919, 1,395gt, 271 feet
Laid down as WAR WEY, but completed as MONTAZAH for the Khedivial Mail Steamship & Graving Dock Co., London, she was one of nine similar C7 standard coasters built between 1919 and 1920. In 1923, she was sold to the Leith, Hull and Hamburg S.P. Co., Leith as FORELAND. In the Currie Line fleet for almost thirty years, she was sold in 1952 and eventually ended up in 1955 as the Israeli ship KISHON. Bought by African Coasters in 1957, on her delivery voyage south as RANGE, she was detained by the Egyptian authorities at Port Said for three months until they were convinced that her new owners really were South Africans. In 1965 she was scrapped in Durban.

BULWARK (bottom)
Dunsmuir & Jackson Ltd., Glasgow; 1920, 1,374gt, 271 feet
African Coasters also owned a sister of RANGE, which was built as MAHMOUDIEH for the Khedivial Mail Steamship & Graving Dock Co., London. She too was bought in 1923 by the Leith, Hull and Hamburg S.P. Co., Leith. Renamed FINLAND, she was not a lucky ship and in 1943 she was beached in the River Tagus after a collision with the Portuguese steamer LIMA (3,881/1907) – refloated, she was repaired in Lisbon. In 1951 she became the Italian owned RUTA and four years later was bought by African Coasters as BULWARK. Like so many South African coasters, her career came to an abrupt end when she was wrecked in 1963 near Danger Point. HMS BIRKENHEAD foundered nearby in 1852 with the loss of 445 lives, but fortunately for those on BULWARK, all were saved.

In the early 1950s, African Coasters purchased three ships which were all originally built for the East African coastal services of three famous shipping companies: Holland Africa Line, Union-Castle Line and British India (BI).

BORDER (top)
N.V. Scheepsbouw Maatschappij "Nieuwe Waterweg", Schiedam, Netherlands; 1923, 886gt, 211 feet
Built for the Holland East Africa Line services of the United Netherlands Company (Vereenigde Nederlandsche Scheepvaartmaatschappij) as HOLLAND, she operated along the East African coast until 1950. The year after she was built, the Holland East Africa Line (names ending in KERK) and the Holland South Africa Line (names ending in FONTEIN) formed a joint round Africa service, known as Holland Africa Line. Sold to African Coasters in 1950 and renamed BORDER, she lasted a further 14 years until she was sold in Durban for scrap. *[Alex Duncan]*

BOUNDARY (middle)
Ardrossan Dockyard Ltd, Ardrossan; 1927, 1,289 gt, 212 feet
Of a similar vintage and size, the twin screw BOUNDARY was originally completed as ROVUMA for the Union-Castle Line. On her delivery voyage to Southern Africa, she towed the new tug ULUNDI to Port Elizabeth – the tug's owners Messina Bros, Coles & Searle had been bought by Union-Castle in 1922. Based in Beira with European officers and African crew, ROVUMA was sold to Colonial Steamships Ltd., Port Louis, Mauritius in 1949 as FLOREAL. With African Coasters from 1954 to 1962, her final moment of fame before being broken up in Durban, was a role in the film *Sanders of the River* starring Richard Todd. *[Alex Duncan]*

VOORLOPER (bottom)
Henry Robb Ltd, Leith; 1937, 1,031 gt, 232 feet
This handsome, engines aft motor coaster was built as SOFALA by Henry Robb for the British India Steam Navigation Company, and was based on a series of similar looking ships ordered for Coast Lines. SOFALA replaced the wrecked DWARKA on the company's East Africa coastal service. During the war she served as a transport and was used in 1941 to carry cased petrol. In 1942, she was the first British merchant ship to enter Benghazi, shortly after its capture by the Allies. Returned to her owners after the war, she served BI for another ten years until her sale to African Coasters in 1955 as VOORLOPER. In 1968 she was sold to Far East owners and was renamed SINCERE ORIENT. Her name was eventually deleted from *Lloyd's Register* in 1993. *[Peter Newall Collection]*

REEF (top)
Burntisland Shipbuilding Co. Ltd., Burntisland; 1937, 1,391gt, 264 feet
Completed in 1937 as EGRET for the British and Continental Steamship Co. Ltd. of Liverpool which traded mainly between UK west coast and Belgium and Dutch ports. Although established in 1922, the company was formed from the ashes of the Cork Steamship Co. Ltd. which had been established in 1872 to operate the continental trade of the original Cork Steamship Co. whose roots went back to the famous St. George Steam Packet Co. of 1821, hence the red cross on a white background houseflag. Their ships were named after birds, and EGRET, first used in the 19th century, was often repeated. A coal burner, she was bought by African Coasters in 1957 and renamed REEF. In 1966, she was sold to Far East owners and was scrapped the following year in Hong Kong. *[Alex Duncan]*

FRONTIER (middle)
John Cockerill S.A., Hoboken, Belgium; 1943, 2,020gt, 288 feet
As WESERSTROM, this was one of nine Hansa A type ships built at various yards in Germany and occupied Europe and allocated to Norddeutscher Lloyd – all had WESER – names and were recognisable by the tall mainmast immediately aft of the superstructure and the kingposts at the forward end. Taken over by the Ministry of War Transport in 1945 as EMPIRE GALENA, she was sold to the General Steam Navigation Co. in 1947 and renamed ALBATROSS. In 1958, she was bought by the short-lived National Shipping Lines of South Africa and briefly had the name PORT CAPETOWN before becoming FRONTIER for African Coasters – interestingly, the previous FRONTIER which was wrecked in 1957 had originally been built for HAPAG. Her final days were spent on the Durban-Indian Ocean trade and in 1966, she was sold to Panamanian buyers and was broken up in 1968. *[Peter Newall Collection]*

VOORSPELER (bottom)
Scott & Sons (Bowling) Ltd., Bowling; 1965, 854gt, 370 feet
Until their merger in 1966 with Smiths Coasters, only three out of the thirty one ships owned by African Coasters had been built for the company. VOORSPELER was the last of these and the final vessel to join the fleet. In October 1974, off Cape St. Francis, she rescued the crew from the stricken tanker TEKTON (15,807/1955) which had been hit amidships in thick fog by the Norwegian OBO QUEEN (54,761/1971). In 1981, she was sold to Panamanian owners and renamed SAGAR. For most of the 1980s, she was laid up in Bangladesh and was scrapped in 1988. *[Peter Newall Collection]*

SMITH'S SUGAR SHIPS

Charles (later Sir Charles) Smith entered the shipping business in 1880 when he chartered the tiny Thames-built tug SOMTSEU to transport sugar from his refinery near Port Shepstone, Natal to Durban. Like African Coasters, Smith's Coasters (Pty.) Ltd., which had been established in 1927, only really took off after the 1954 abolition of the sea competitive rates scheme, although the company had built in the late 1930s two ships (GAMTOOS and NAHOON) specially for the sugar trade.

MEAD (top)
Smith's Dock Co. Ltd., Middlesbrough; 1919, 606gt,170 feet
The initial fleet of Smith's Coasters (Pty.) Ltd. included two converted 'Kil' class patrol gunboats, HOMEFORD and MEAD which were bought in 1927. Designed with a similar shaped bow and stern and dazzle painted to confuse the enemy as to which direction was being steamed, over 50 of these ships were built in 1918 and 1919, mainly by Smith's Dock. Originally HMS KILMEAD, she was given a new bow and raised forecastle when transformed into a merchant ship in 1920. In 1942, she was requisitioned by the Admiralty and converted into a cable layer for the harbour defences at Cape Town, Durban and Port Elizabeth. Taken over by the South African Navy in 1944, at the end of hostilities, MEAD recovered most of the valuable cable she had laid. When she returned to her owners in 1947, she had been virtually rebuilt and continued on the sugar routes for another ten years until she was sold to a Durban concern as KOMATI. In 1960, she was scrapped in Durban.

INYONI (middle)
Howaldtswerke A.G., Hamburg, Germany; 1938, 1,223gt, 251 feet
Smith's Coasters also owned two handsome ex-German ships which were built for the well-known Bremen short sea company, Argo Reederei (Argo Line) just before the war. When barely a year old, SCHWAN was taken over by the German Navy as the patrol boat V 101, and in 1940 was converted into a minefield breaker SPERRBRECHER 31 (in 1941, this number was increased to 131) based in Aarhus, Denmark. Because of the constant danger from air attacks, the ship was smothered in dazzle paint and, in case she struck a mine, her holds were filled with empty barrels to prevent her sinking. Somehow, she managed to survive the war unscathed and was handed over to the Ministry of War Transport who sold her in 1948 to Atkinson & Prickett Ltd. who renamed her WELTONWOLD. After a spell with Currie Line, Leith as RHINELAND from 1949 to 1956, she became HERRIESBROOK, prior to her sale to Smith's Coasters in 1957. Withdrawn in 1961, she was sold to Durban breakers. *[Alex Duncan]*

INDUNA (bottom)
Nordseewerke Emden G.m.b.H., Emden, Germany; 1938, 1,214gt, 247 feet
With her unmistakable flared bow, HABICHT was completed a few months earlier than SCHWAN, but was not so lucky during the war as she was sunk at Libau in 1944. Salvaged in 1945, she was taken to Kiel for repairs and was again sunk. Raised a second time after the war, she was allocated to Holland as a war reparation. Rebuilt, she was sold in 1948 to the N.V. Maatschappij Zeevart, Rotterdam as HAGNO. Smith's Coasters bought her in 1954 and she remained with the company until 1962 when she was scrapped. *[Peter Newall Collection]*

SMALLER COMPANIES

In the post-war years, numerous companies came and went as speculators tried to make money in this difficult trade.

BOKKEVELD (top)
Dunlop & Bremner Co. Ltd., Port Glasgow; 1919, 2,481gt, 303 feet
Completed as BACKWORTH for the short sea fleet of the Newcastle tramp company R.S.Dalgleish Ltd., this ship ended her days as a hulk on Cape Town's Eastern Mole. In 1939 she was sold to the Branch Steamship Co. of Cardiff and renamed OGMORE CASTLE and in 1946 was bought by the newly-formed Arden Hall Steamship Co. of Cape Town as BOKKEVELD. Used as far as Matadi, her limited power meant that she struggled against the flow of the Congo River. With the collapse of the company in 1951, she was sold to another short-lived venture, Van Riebeeck Lines, and renamed ROODEWAL before her final sale to Senator Sam Pettersen in 1954. Senator Pettersen was an eccentric who bought a number of ancient ships in the mid-1950s, including the 1897 Thesen's ship CLARA. None of these ships were used much and lay rusting at their berths with the Senator refusing to pay any harbour dues. ROODEWAL became part of the 'ghost fleet' as it was known locally and was eventually scrapped in 1963. *[Peter Newall Collection]*

K. RAPANOS (middle)
Ropner & Sons, Stockton-on-Tees; 1912, 1,114gt, 215 feet
Of all the coastal ships operating along the South African Coast, this was probably the most unusual. Built as the PORT OF LONDON AUTHORITY HOPPER No. 23, she was later renamed JAMES No. 66. In 1938, she was bought by South African Railways and Harbours as NEWEY to transport mud dredged from Durban Bay and dump it beyond the breakwater. In 1946, the newly formed Neptune Shipping Company bought this hopper and had her converted into an oil-fired coaster at the local Dorman Long shipyard. As the unfortunately named K. RAPANOS, she traded mainly to the Indian Ocean Islands until her sale to Italian buyers in 1952, and was broken up in 1960. *[Peter Newall Collection]*

ALIWAL (bottom)
W. Harkess & Son Ltd., Middlesbrough; 1920, 1,425gt, 235 feet
Another of Senator Pettersen's purchases was this interesting engines-aft ship, with a well deck forward. One of only four C6 standard coasters built, she was laid down as WAR BURE and completed as ENUGU for the Government of Nigeria. In 1943, she was bought by the Ministry of War Transport and renamed EMPIRE LIDDELL, with Elder Dempster Lines as managers. She too was purchased by the ill-fated Arden Hall Steamship Co. in 1947 (as HOËVELD) and, in 1951, was sold to Van Riebeeck Lines as ALIWAL. In 1954, she became part of the Pettersen fleet and was based in Durban. Declared unseaworthy by the Marine Division (her lifeboats were full of holes!), she spent the last five years of her life laid up in Durban until she was sent to the breakers yard in 1961. *[Peter Newall Collection]*

INDEX TO RECORD 5 TO 8

Record 5: pp.1-64; *Record 6*: pp.65-128; *Record 7*: pp.129-192; *Record 8*: pp.193-264.

Index of articles

Index of ships

ISBN 1-901703-02-9

9 781901 703023 >

Ships in Focus Publications

£6.00